Lit Crit Guides

Reading and Interpreting the Works of

MARK TWAIN

Spring Hermann

This book is dedicated to my husband, Vincent Gagliardi, and to all my friends in Connecticut who generously support the Mark Twain House and Museum.

I wish to acknowledge and thank for sharing their vast knowledge of Mark Twain and for taking great professional care of his former homes and legacy: Cindy Lovell, executive director of the Mark Twain House and Museum, Hartford, Connecticut, and Henry H. Sweets III, director of the Mark Twain Boyhood Home and Museum, Hannibal, Missouri.

Published in 2018 by Enslow Publishing, LLC
101 W. 23rd Street, Suite 240, New York, NY 10011

Cataloging-in-Publication Data
Names: Hermann, Spring.
Title: Reading and interpreting the works of Mark Twain / Spring Hermann.
Description: New York : Enslow Publishing, 2018 | Series: Lit crit guides | Includes bibliographical references and index. | Audience: Grades 7-12.
Identifiers: ISBN 9780766084933 (library bound)
Subjects: LCSH: Twain, Mark, 1835-1910--Criticism and interpretation--Juvenile literature. | Twain, Mark, 1835-1910--Juvenile literature.
Classification: LCC PS1342.H55 Z678 2018 | DDC 813.409--dc23

Printed in China

10 9 8 7 6 5 4 3 2 1

To Our Readers: We have done our best to make sure all website addresses in this book were active and appropriate when we went to press. However, the author and the publisher have no control over and assume no liability for the material available on those websites or on any websites they may link to. Any comments or suggestions can be sent by email to customerservice@enslow.com.

Photo Credits: Cover, p. 3 Topical Press Agency/Hulton Archive/Getty Images; p. 6 Hulton Archive/Getty Images; pp. 9, 100 Everett Historical/Shutterstock.com; p. 14 Weldon Schloneger/Shutterstock.com; pp. 18, 81 Corbis/Getty Images2; pp. 23, 105 GraphicaArtis/Archive Photos/Getty Images; pp. 26, 55, 64, 71 Culture Club/Hulton Archive/Getty Images; pp. 31, 88 Print Collector/Hulton Archive/Getty Images; pp. 33, 41 Bettmann/Hulton Archive/Getty Images; p. 36 Charles Phelps Cushing/ClassicStock/Archive Photos/Getty Images; p. 44 Danita Delimont/Alamy Stock Photo; p. 48 Transcendental Graphics/Archive Photos/Getty Images; p. 58 Fotosearch/Archive Photos/Getty Images; p. 61 Universal History Archive/Universal Images Group/Getty Images; p. 75 Historical Picture Archive/Corbis/Getty Images; p. 94 Rischgitz/Hulton Archive/Getty Images; p. 112 ITAR-TASS Photo Agency/Alamy Stock Photo; p. 115 AF archive/Alamy Stock Photo; p. 120 f11photo/Shutterstock.com; p. 124 Popartic/Shutterstock.com.

CONTENTS

Mark Twain

A Boy Survives on the Western Frontier

All the Clemens men had gifts, talents, learning, and a deep drive to make a profit. Alas, none of them seemed to have any luck.

John Marshall Clemens left his father's family plantation in Virginia as a boy after his father died a financial failure. He resettled in Kentucky, where he married Jane Lampton. They moved to Tennessee to take over a large land investment, which did not make them a profit. The couple had a son, Orion, and two daughters, Pamela and Margaret. A brother-in-law raved about opportunities in Missouri—the nearest territory on the frontier where you could bring your slaves. The Clemens family moved west, where they bought land and shared a farm in Florida, Missouri. The farm would fail to make enough profit to keep them all.

It was in this village that Samuel Langhorne Clemens was "born two months premature, on November 30, 1835."[1] Since Jane Clemens had already lost an infant son back in Tennessee, and believed her tiny, sickly baby Sammy would not pull through, she became deeply depressed. She could not know that this son Samuel had it in him to survive not only his frightening birth but many other injuries and scrapes with death throughout his long and often risky existence.

Samuel's grandparents, his parents, and his brother would all struggle to become wealthy, respected, secure, even powerful in their worlds. For the most part, they failed to achieve these goals. Although Samuel would also make failed attempts at obtaining wealth and power, he did one thing that none of them could begin to do.

He became a successful writer under the pseudonym Mark Twain.

From the Prairie to the River: Sammy's Worlds Change

In 1839, Sammy's father, John, made a deal for a city block in Hannibal, Missouri, a newly chartered village on the Mississippi River. John and Jane desperately wanted a new start, for another tragedy had befallen the family. Sammy had endured his touch-and-go infancy and was almost four, thanks in large part to the nursing of Jenny, their last slave. While Sammy lived in decent health, their beloved daughter Margaret was felled by yellow fever, a virus of the liver, and died at age nine. (It was Margaret's tragic fate to be bitten by an infected mosquito that never bit her five siblings.) In part to put their grief behind them, John and Jane packed up Orion (fourteen), Pamela (twelve), Benjamin (seven), Sammy (four), and new baby Henry (sixteen months), and departed for Hannibal. Sammy was leaving behind the climate and sights and smells of the prairie for a nearby new world: the banks of the Mississippi River.

The Clemens family settled in as respected Hannibal citizens, although they had to live economically. Young Sam went to dame school (today's nursery school) and then a primary school. His parents were literate and supported his studies at home. Yet by the age of five, Sam was already a wanderer, fond of exploring life on and off the great river. He wrote later of what he termed the "hungry Mississippi": "[Its] mile wide breadth of water seemed an ocean to [the children]...and the vague riband of trees on the further shore, the verge of a continent which surely none but they had ever seen before."[2]

A short walk from home down to the riverbank—often made unaccompanied—exposed little Sam to an amazing array of boats and passengers. Into his memory were

Mark Twain visits his boyhood home in Hannibal.

embedded images of immense white steamboats with their paddle wheels, lush furnishings, blasting whistles and calliope music, and mounds of cotton bales stacked on lower decks. And what a cast of characters they provided: southern planters with their perfectly gowned wives, foreign merchants and immigrants up from New Orleans, fancy-dressed gamblers, soldiers, prostitutes, actors, and trappers with guns strapped to their hips. Sam took them in, listened to them, longed in some way to be part of them—and by age nine had already tried to stow away! Smaller fishing boats and ferry rafts also impressed him. It may have already entered his imagination that if boys could get hold of one, they might ride the great river themselves.

In May 1842, another sibling was lost to Sam—his nine-year-old brother Benjamin. He too became sick with yellow fever, and like his sister Margaret, could not be saved. Sam felt guilty for some reason. When his mother made him caress Benjamin's cheek in his coffin as a sign of farewell, seven-year-old Sam felt a sense of loss from which he never recovered.

Sam's Relationships with Pals and Slaves

By eight or nine years old, Sam hooked up with two boys who loved playing hooky and taking risks as much as he did. Will Bowen and Tom Blankenship became his devoted buddies. Tom was older, poor, and undisciplined. Will was a bit younger, and followed Sam's lead in adventures. Years later when Sam became a major author, Will and Tom, given different names, served as several of his greatest fictional characters.

A neighborhood girl, Anna Laura Hawkins, was the first object of Sam's affection. Later he would use her as a model for the appealing young females in several of his books. Laura recalled Sam as having fuzzy red curls all over his head, "That really ought to have belonged to a girl."[3] She claimed that she and Sam played together like two girls, indicating that Sam saved his crazy, risky pranks for his boy "gang," but treated Laura like a sister as well as his sweetheart. Laura also noted that although Sam's family was poor, he always shared his candy and fruit with her. She remembered Sam's "drawling, appealing voice" when he told amusing stories.[4]

Undoubtedly Laura and Sam shared a love of reading the great books of the 1840s, and were literary comrades. When it came to the boy gang members, Sam had to teach them the lines from the tales of Robin Hood, as well as the works of early American authors—lines which Sam had the remarkable ability to memorize. Then they would recreate the exploits of these characters, especially the violent parts.

To help the usually cash strapped Clemens family, Sam's older sister Pamela used her talents for singing and playing piano and guitar to give lessons. Sam was one of her most avid pupils. He sang and played with proficiency for the rest of his life. Sam also loved the music and drama provided by traveling shows. With his hoarded coins, ten-year-old Sam bought tickets to the minstrel shows. Thomas "Daddy" Rice, the star song-and-dance man, performed in blackface makeup the ludicrous, exaggerated black character he named "Jim Crow." Like most boys who came from slave-holding families, Sam knew this performance was a joke. Black men did not behave this way. However, he thought it so funny that he used to imitate Jim Crow himself, sometimes even as an adult.

Although John Clemens eventually had to sell off his slaves to pay his debts, Sam did develop close relationships with slaves over the summers that he spent on his uncle John Quarles's farm. Sam recalled later, "He had eight children and fifteen or twenty negroes...I have not come across a better man than he was."[5]

The Quarles farm mainly grew tobacco, the planting, harvesting, and curing of which was the hard job of those who lived in "the negro quarters."[6] The young slaves became Sam's comrades, although they always called him "Mars [Master] Sam." Certain slaves, such as Aunt Hannah (who was an expert in superstitions and practiced witchery) and hardworking Uncle Daniel, became icons in Sam's heart. He later wrote that during these summers "I got my strong liking for [Daniel's] race, and my appreciation for certain of its fine qualities. This feeling and this estimate have stood the test of sixty years...the black face is as welcome to me now as it was then."[7] No one among Sam's relatives or friends, all of whom were masters and regular churchgoers, ever told him that slavery was evil. During the 1840s and 1850s, the Presbyterian Church of Hannibal, the Clemens's own congregation, passed out tracts published in the South. They explained that the institution of black slavery was God's will for his people.

Sam did notice on several occasions that his mother, Jane, felt the tragedy of owning a young slave boy named Sandy. This boy's family was split up and left behind on the Maryland shore, while Sandy ended up in Hannibal. It bothered Sam that Sandy sang and whistled and even laughed so much, seemingly for no reason. Jane told Sam that Sandy was using these verbal devices to keep from thinking. "He will never see his mother again. If he can sing, I must not hinder it, but be thankful for it...that friendless child's noise [s]hould make you glad."[8] What finally became of Sandy, Sam never seemed to know.

After slavery had been abolished, Sam looked back at his youth in Hannibal and attempted to justify his family's slave ownership. He reflected that slavery in that region "was the mild domestic slavery, not the brutal plantation article."[9] He noted that cruelties were rare, and to separate a family by selling them off was disliked by the people and seldom done. Sam admitted that he did see "a dozen black men and women chained to one another once, lying on the pavement, awaiting shipment to the Southern slave market. These were the saddest faces I have ever seen."[10] The older he grew, the more conflicted Sam became about slavery as an institution. He reflected on his kind-hearted mother's long life as an owner: "I think she was not conscious that slavery was a bald, grotesque, unwarrantable usurpation."[11]

Sam's Growing Passion for Risk

Between the ages of ten and twelve, Sam and his pals graduated into trying more dangerous stunts. A favorite activity was sneaking around Hannibal at night. Sam was able to leave his bedmate Henry soundly asleep, drop out of the window onto the roof, then to the shed, and down to his waiting friends. Drunks, river bums, tramps, and thieves also roamed the village, making it doubly unwise for young boys to go around unprotected. Fights and even shootings occurred day and night. Yet Sam and the boys managed to find haunted houses in which to peek, clearings in the woods where they could make campfires, and ships docked on the river to explore. Often existing on half a night's sleep, it is clear why Sam— although a brilliant child—did mediocre work in school.

A favorite stunt for Sam and the gang was to "borrow" a small boat and paddle it across the Mississippi toward the Illinois shore. Although the current could be treacherous, the gang always made it to "the shallow waters of Bird Slough, a sandy stretch between Sny Island and Illinois Territory."[12]

The boys learned that they could pick wild blackberries and pecans, which they feasted upon. On one trip in August 1847, the boys made a frightening discovery in the shallow waters of Bird Slough: the corpse of an escaped slave rose up and floated toward them. Terrified of the corpse's "spirit," the boys madly paddled back across to Hannibal. The true story eventually came out: Tom Blankenship's older brother Bence had discovered the slave hiding on the Illinois island, took pity on him, and brought him stolen food. But Bence could not figure out how to save the man, who was eventually caught and murdered by Illinois wood cutters.

The mighty Mississippi River as it looks now

Sam's Boyhood Ends

The Clemens family had to give up their house on Virginia Street—their boarders had failed to pay the rent and so the Clemens family could no longer afford the house. John Clemens also lost his general store, as too many folks bought on credit and never paid up. The work he got as a lawyer and judge fed the family. In 1847 John headed home on horseback from a trip on court business, got hit by a sleet storm, and caught pneumonia. Orion, then apprenticed in St. Louis, made it home to his father's bedside, along with Pamela, Sam, and Henry. John died at age forty-nine, almost completely broke. He died about ten years too soon. Historian Ron Powers tells us that when the railroad made it to Hannibal, "it ushered in a boom town epoch that lasted three quarters of a century."[13]

Sam was still eleven, not quite old enough to be apprenticed in 1847. So when not in school, he ran errands, clerked for the grocer, and delivered the Hannibal newspaper. His free days of playing hooky were over. One year later, Sam swore that he would work hard and dutifully as an apprentice, if his mother swore she would never make him attend formal school again. So Sam joined the world of journalism, where he did basic shop labor at the newspaper and learned to set type. Sam's fascination for printing and publishing was born and would last his entire life. As he began to read the stories he was typesetting, he knew that someday he would be writing them.

By 1849 Sam was setting up stories on the California Gold Rush and the horrific cholera epidemic that was spread by traffic coming upriver from New Orleans. As the newspapers' owners ran off to avoid disease—and find gold—Sam's brother Orion, who had been working in the business in St. Louis, purchased their two newspapers. From them he created one paper: the *Hannibal Western Union*. His first hire was Sam.

As Sam moved through his teen years he learned to write, edit, and use satire. Many times he personally "put the paper out" because Orion was busy or unwell. Younger brother Henry Clemens joined as an apprenticed staff member. Sam started in 1851 to write pieces of frontier satire and send them to large papers on the East Coast. He also began to master what was called "darky humor," the made-up dialogue that sounded a lot like the minstrel shows. By his seventeenth birthday, Sam had fashioned a career in news writing and editing. When Orion and his wife, Mollie, returned to work in St. Louis, Sam followed. Sam's sister Pamela had married a St. Louis citizen and made her home there too.

> **satire**
>
> A piece of writing that makes fun of a person or idea.

But Sam's secret dream still haunted him, a dream he did not know how to fulfill. He longed for serious adventure—past the boyhood risks of haunted houses, woodland hideouts, dark deep caves, and moonlit trips to islands across the Mississippi. He was twenty-one when suddenly a fifty-dollar bill blew along the street in Keokuk, Iowa, where he'd been working. No one claimed the lost note. Sam wrote in his memoirs, "I felt I must take that money out of danger. So I bought a ticket to Cincinnati."[14]

It would be now or never, Sam decided. After working for Cincinnati's printing companies, he invested the rest of his money and boarded a river packet (a small boat) sailing to New Orleans. When he landed, to his surprise, he was handed a chance to have that adventure and fulfill his dream.

Sam's Boyhood Lives Again: *The Adventures of Tom Sawyer*

Samuel Clemens's boyhood effectively ended wth his father's death in 1847. Sam turned twelve at that time and had to go to work. Almost exactly thirty years later, after sketching ideas for a long time about using his youth as fictional material, Sam [by then writing as Mark Twain] wrote the preface to a novel he had just completed. He claimed "most of the adventures recorded in this book really occurred; one or two were experiences of my own, the rest those of boys who were schoolmates of mine. Huck Finn is drawn from life; Tom Sawyer also."[1]

For Sam's friends from Hannibal who shared those adventures, it must have been amazing to read them in *The Adventures of Tom Sawyer*! Perhaps they assumed most of their bad deeds would remain buried with their own childhoods. They could easily separate the fictional elements from the raucous recountings with which Sam filled his novel. Yet for the rest of *Tom Sawyer*'s readership, which spread around the country and the world, reality and fiction blended so perfectly that they did not wish to separate them, but merely to do as Mr. Twain wanted. He intended the novel to be mainly for the entertainment of young people, yet "it was part of my plan to

Sam Clemens at age fifteen. By this time he had dropped out of school and held a job as an apprentice to a printer.

try to pleasantly remind adults of what they once were themselves, of how they felt and thought and talked."[2]

When Sam wrote the bulk of this novel, he was living in Hartford, Connecticut, and summering in Elmira, New York. It was a decade after America had survived the War Between The States, as the Civil War was known in the South. We may wonder, how had Hannibal changed? First, Missouri, a state which had been considered borderline Confederate, took a beating in the war. Many of the young men Sam knew might have been wounded or killed. Most important, slavery became illegal in every state. Yet small town society had not changed much, both north and south. It was fairly easy to remind adults about what and who they once were.

The Central Characters of Tom's World

Tom Sawyer's family consists of his late mother's sister, Aunt Polly; a half brother, Sidney; and a cousin, Mary. Tom's parents are deceased. His inner circle consists of his best buddies, Joe Harper and Ben Rodgers; his sweetheart, Becky Thatcher; and his slightly older, wilder friend called Huckleberry Finn. Huck is disliked by all the town's parents for being without discipline or manners, even bad. Alfred the rich boy is the main pain in Tom's side.

The adult community of St. Petersburg (the alias for Hannibal) also figures heavily in the plot: Injun Joe, a criminal half breed; Muff Potter, a well-meaning drunken thief; Mr. Dobbins, the brutal school master; and kindly Widow Douglas who tries to help Huck. All these people attempt to influence Tom for bad or good.

We are never given Tom's exact age, but he appears to be about eleven, the age when Sam Clemens had to go to work. Flowing between boyhood and adolescence, stuck in some strange period of risky games and fantasies, Tom is just starting to comprehend the evils and dangers of the grownup world. Tom's gang plays games as robbers and pirates—only to have the dangers of these adult activities come alive, suck them in, and almost destroy them.

Levels of Meaning in Tom's Story

This novel should first be read just for fun. The reader needs to absorb its delightful trip through mid-nineteenth-century small town America. Tom, Joe, Ben, and Huck play marbles, pretend to pilot a steamboat, feign illness to skip school, put together a make-believe minstrel band, and design war campaigns with Tom and Joe as opposing generals. These games are relatively harmless products of boyish imagination. Tom even persuades his sweetheart to Becky go through an "engagement ceremony" with him—a delightful peek into adult love without any of its true consequences.

Most of these activities are based on Sam's early memories. His rendition of a boyhood summer in Hannibal, although free from the dreaded schoolroom, shows how uninteresting real life could become. For example, "The Glorious Fourth" procession which Tom adored gets rained out. The guest speaker does arrive. "The greatest man in the world (as Tom supposed) Mr. [Thomas Hart] Benton, an actual United States Senator, proved an overwhelming disappointment—for he was not twenty-five feet high, not even anywhere in the neighborhood of it."[3] A circus comes, a phrenologist and a mesmerizer perform, but when they leave the village seems hot and boring. To make the season even worse for Tom, Becky Thatcher is taken to the family's other home for the summer. As if in response to this, Tom comes down with the hard measles, a dangerous disease which then required bed rest.

However, Tom and his buddy Huckleberry Finn have already endured an event that will not leave Tom's mind. Together they witnessed a grave robbery and a murder. We aren't sure that such a grisly experience actually happened to Sam, but grave robbing was common in this period. In *Tom Sawyer*, the village physician, Doctor Robinson, pays Injun Joe and Muff Potter, two men on the fringe of society, to dig up a corpse—presumably for dissection practice. Caught hiding in the graveyard during one of their crazy superstitious rituals, Tom and Huck witness the revealing of the casket, then the quarrel between Muff and Dr. Robinson, who beans Muff with a grave tablet and gets stabbed himself in a fight with Injun Joe. When Robinson dies, Injun Joe revives Muff and convinces him he killed the doctor in a struggle, but does not remember because he was drunk as usual.

The boys have entered a new level of meaning: the real evil in life. The game of dodging ghosts and treasure hunting in a graveyard pales in comparison to the actual terror they have witnessed. They know that Injun Joe is the true killer and Muff Potter just an accomplice. They have seen enough to hang Injun Joe. After racing back to the village, Tom and Huck debate their future if they confess the truth.

> Tom says, "Suppose something happened and Indian Joe didn't hang? Why he'd kill us some time or other, dead sure as we're laying here."

> Huck agrees, then observes, "If anybody tells, let Muff do it. He's fool enough. He's generally drunk enough." But Tom realizes that because he was knocked out, "Muff Potter doesn't know it." Tom notes that Muff may even die from his head wound.

Huck's reply is one of the most telling of this character's young life. He doubts that the drunken Muff will die of his wound, because he compares Muff to his own father Pap Finn:

> "When pap's full, you might take and belt him over the head with a church and you couldn't phase him. He says so his own self."[4]

Although Tom knows what it is to be fatherless, at that moment he must realize that Huckleberry Finn's situation with his violent, derelict dad is even more miserable. The boys write an oath of mutual secrecy and sign it in blood. This childish response to an extremely dangerous adult situation shows the reader that Tom is trying to cope with his fear of Injun Joe, his conflicting sense of moral responsibility, and own self-preservation.

Symbolism in *Tom Sawyer*

A series of experiences both funny and frightening make up the contents of *Tom Sawyer*. Many show Tom as a clever boy filled with imagination and what his aunt calls "sass." The famed scene in which Tom's pals beg to whitewash Aunt Polly's fence finds Tom using the huckster's skills he learned by listening to the barkers

symbolism

Using one thing to stand for, represent, or suggest something else.

that promote the circuses and shows that traveled through Hannibal. Making a captive "pet" of a tick, a pinch bug, a bat, or a snake demonstrates Tom's fondness for nature and his ability to amuse himself in a poor family.

Tom cons friends into whitewashing Aunt Polly's fence.

The Island

However, the use of what was called Jackson's Island on the far side of the Mississippi takes on a larger meaning. Twain writes about the island as a pirate's hideout, but the Hannibal boys of his youth used it as a getaway. With stolen food, utensils, and fishing gear, the "pirates" in the novel head for a secret campout. They are so angry at their families for various reasons that they fail to consider what their absence for days and nights will mean to them. They endure a Mississippi River whopper of a thunderstorm, then run out of food, and finally get homesick.

Jackson's Island symbolizes a place where the boys try to get away from their society's rules, and be powerful and independent. Tom also wants his family to be sorry for mistreating him, so he runs away for this purpose. The final scene of this story arc finds the boys coming back into St. Petersburg to find everyone in church weeping. They end up attending their own funeral service, for it is assumed the three boys have drowned in the storm.

The Cave

McDougal's Cave, also a real place in Sam Clemens's childhood, plays another interesting role. The cave was a hot spot for both children and adults to explore and enjoy the creepy thrills of the dark underground. The rules of cave exploration always revolve around safety—especially in this one. Twain describes it as "miles in extent…a tangled wilderness of narrow lofty clefts and passages. It was an easy place to get lost in."[5]

Cave exploration in the 1840s was done with candles and lit torches, and attempts to scratch identifying marks and autographs on the walls. When Tom Sawyer leads Becky

Thatcher down with a cave party, it's a sure bet he will try to show off for her—as usual—and take them down an untrod path. (A similar incident happened to young Sam. Fortunately, he and his girlfriend were rescued by a search party just as their candle nearly burned out.) Twain takes Tom Sawyer one step farther, and has him discover, Indiana Jones-style, a new exit from the cave, just in time to save Becky's life.

There are several ideas about what the cave may have meant to Tom—and to Sam Clemens. It provides a place for Tom to summon up a level of courage and affection for Becky that shows us he is maturing. But is it more than a dramatic setting? Twain also uses the cave as Injun Joe's hideout where he buries his loot. So that young people never get lost in the cave again, the townspeople board it up completely. The exotic hideout becomes Injun Joe's tomb. An outcast who always went against the rules of society finds himself unable to be rescued from the place he used to live his life of crime.

Tom and Huck Endure the Consequences of Riches

In Sam Clemens's own youth, he scrambled for every cent he could earn to help keep his family going. Tom and Huck, being fictional versions, could have any sort of ending to their remarkable summer that Mark Twain wished. So he granted them an amazing treasure in the sum of $12,000 in gold coins—found loot that is split between the boys.

In Tom's case, having the money makes Aunt Polly's life so much easier that Tom is pleased with his situation. But Huckleberry, who has been taken in by the Widow Douglas, finds that fortune brings stifling expectations. He has to eat, drink, dress, and speak like a proper young man. Twain observed, "The bars and shackles of civilization shut him in and bound

Act. 1.
=
Scene 1.
=
A village cottage, with back
door looking into garden.
A closet + the ordinary
furniture. Old lady of
50, cheaply + neatly dressed.
Wears spectacles—knitting.

= (The old lady)
Aunt Winny.—Tom!

[to answer.] Tom! [to
answer.] What's gone with
that boy, I wonder? You

A handwritten first draft of *Tom Sawyer*, which was first written as a play him hand and foot."[6] After three weeks, Huck vanishes, to resume his slovenly ways.

In short, Twain finds the boys at odds. Tom sees that great financial gain can bring responsibility but also the option to buy life's better things. On the other hand, Huck learns that a great deal of money can ruin his completely carefree life on the edge of society.

What should we make of the book's ending? It appears Tom and Huck seek the middle road. They will live a decent life with Aunt Polly and the Widow Douglas, but they will also find time to take up with their old "robber gang." They will live with one foot still in boyhood and the other toe touching the maturity of adulthood.

In the novel's conclusion, Mark Twain muses that most of these characters' prototypes are still alive, prosperous, and happy. "Some day it may seem worth while to take up the story of the younger ones again," he says, perhaps the kernel of the great future novel *Adventures of Huckleberry Finn* taking root in his mind.[7]

Critics Praise *The Adventures of Tom Sawyer*

According to the historians of the University of Virginia Twain collection, Mark Twain may have lived the story of Tom Sawyer in the 1840s, but he did not write it until the 1870s. It was finished in January 1876, but publishers' confusions about how to market it, plus a pirated (illegally copied) edition in Canada, caused the book to be delayed. (Yes, the "pirate" Tom Sawyer became the "pirated" Mark Twain.)

When the critics finally got hold of the novel, they saw that Tom Sawyer was "Every Boy." The 1876 review in the *Atlantic Monthly* by William Dean Howells says, "He is mischievous but not vicious; he is ready for almost any depredation that

1840S SLANG IN *TOM SAWYER*

The following are only a few of the colloquial expressions used by the folks of St. Petersburg, Missouri. See if you can guess their meaning. The answers are below.

1. "Never did see the beat of that boy."
2. "What is that truck?"
3. "He's full of the old Scratch"
4. "No more of your sass"
5. "Headboard"
6. "Bully!"; "they have just a bully time"
7. "Mum's the word." "Keep mum."

1. No one can top that boy for mischief; 2. Truck meant a small commodity, here it refers to the smeared jam around Tom's mouth; 3. Old Scratch meant the Devil or Satan; 4. Sass meant rudeness or backtalk; 5. A headboard—in a graveyard— was a small stone tablet-style marker; 6. Bully! meant Great! or Fantastic! (far from today's meaning of a cruel person); 7. Mum meant to keep information private, unspoken.

involves danger and the honor of adventure... he resorts to any stratagem to keep out of school, but he is never a downright liar... although every boy has wild and fantastic dreams, this boy cannot rest till he has somehow realized them."[8]

A London critic caught a lot of the amusement throughout the book. "A great deal of Mark Twain's humor consists in the serious—or even at times severe—style in which he narrates his stories and portrays his scenes."[9] This critic also noted the magnitude of the book. "There is something stately, in the simplicity with which [Twain] invites us to turn our attention to the affairs of some boys and girls growing up on the far frontiers of American civilization."

Finally the *New York Times* rang in with an unsigned review that revealed the writer's fascination with the authenticity of all the book's characters. "Tom is a preternaturally precocious urchin. One admirable character in the book, touched with the hand of a master [author] is that of Huckleberry Finn. There is a reality about this boy which is striking."[10]

colloquial
Having to do with informal conversation; how people talk.

The Adventures of Tom Sawyer became a classic, one of the first crossover novels to find success with both children and their parents. Today well over twenty million copies have sold.

SAM TAKES CHARGE
OF A LARGER BOAT

In the spring of 1854, Sam Clemens became a wandering printer journalist. Although his primary job was setting the type for print jobs, he also began to cover stories for newspapers. He took printshop jobs in St. Louis, then in other cities up and down the Mississippi and Ohio Rivers. Not even twenty years of age, Sam had become a rambler, a lone rover, a young man who did not yet understand what was driving him.

When he traveled to and from these cities, Clemens rode the steamboats that took travelers and goods on the midwestern rivers. Each journey must have reminded him of the excitement he felt as a boy running down to the Hannibal docks to see the paddle wheelers arrive, even "borrowing" someone's skiff and paddling across the wide Mississippi to his island getaways. That excitement could happen every day if he could actually pilot a boat!

Clemens's impossible dream suddenly came true. Historian Forrest Robinson says when Clemens arrived in New Orleans in 1857, "he met Horace Bixby, a veteran steamboat pilot, who agreed to take him on as an apprentice (or cub) pilot for $500."[1] Clemens found the money and started the difficult training course, which meant handling the humblest jobs serving the pilot. He referred to Mr. Bixby as his owner during the two year apprenticeship. He worked his way up until he finally memorized the entire Mississippi from St. Louis to New Orleans, all its channels and turns and islands and docks. With none of today's instruments such as sonar and scientific river charts and super headlights, Sam steered the big ship. He could even navigate it in the dark, having sharp eyesight and a poleman call out the depths of the riverbed, which often changed.

A steamboat docked on the Mississippi River in the mid-1800s. The top cabin held the steering wheel where the pilot stood.

Sam's Years as a Master Pilot

Clemens became a licensed and respected river boat pilot. It was just as interesting a life as he had imagined. However, steamboats could have catastrophic accidents. Years later Mark Twain wrote about such a catastrophe in his book *Life on the Mississippi*, and relived it in his *Autobiography*. Sam had helped get an apprenticeship for his young brother Henry, who had no employment or sense of direction. Together they served on the *Pennsylvania*. When the steamboat docked in New Orleans, Sam and Henry parted—Sam was to crew another ship that would leave two days later. On the way back up to Memphis, the *Pennsylvania*'s boilers exploded—as well as a cargo of flammable liquid—and all the crew and passengers were blasted with steam and flames. Henry Clemens was one of the crew aboard. Over one hundred and fifty people were reported dead. Henry was mortally wounded but did survive long enough for his brother Sam to make it to his Memphis hospital bed. Sam never got over the guilt of helping put Henry on that ship—even though Henry's death was just a tragic accident.

Sam Clemens continued to work as a steamboat pilot, for it somehow helped him get through his grief for Henry. He earned good pay, much of which he put in the bank. He swore he did not gamble, but had many adventures during his breaks at the rivers' ports.

Once in a while Clemens made a mistake or two. In the summer of 1860, biographer Ron Powers reports, Clemens was steering "the huge *City of Memphis*...awaiting orders to 'back' from his captain whom he thought he could see from the corner of his eye. The shape turned out to be the captain's coat draped over the big bell."[2] The order never came, and the

Samuel Clemens's precious pilot's license, dated April 9, 1859 ship banged into the New Orleans levee. No real harm was done except to Clemens's pride. Looking back, he even saw the humor in it. He would stash this incident, along with countless others about the river, and use them in his future books.

The Civil War Threatens the River Trade

Clemens got involved at this time with other young men on the ships who wanted to argue over the possible secession of the Southern states. He was a Missourian, stubborn, and yet wavering in his view. Mostly he still wanted the Union to survive. When Abraham Lincoln of Illinois ran for the presidency that year, Sam's brother Orion campaigned for him in hostile northern Missouri. Lincoln did win, narrowly, which set off the secession of seven Southern states. Missouri remained on the borderline, still in the Union, but allowing slavery.

In 1861, commercial river boating was shut down by the onset of the Civil War. Each side tried to gain control over the rivers and their ports. This left Sam Clemens without a job or a purpose in life. He was rightfully afraid he might get commandeered to pilot government gunboats. Since he was so conflicted about the war, that was the last thing he wanted to do.

Forrest Robinson said, "Clemens returned to Hannibal in June 1861 and helped organize...a ragtag troop of volunteers."[3] In the early years of the Civil War, volunteer militias made up the majority of the troops. Men were expected to wear their own fighting clothes, bring their guns, and hopefully a horse or mule to ride. Clemens's Hannibal-area militia joined the Missouri state guards, intending to fight off the Federals in Jefferson City. He believed in the Union but still did not want to fight on either side. Ron Powers tells a funny story about this situation. Clemens and two friends were sitting near the Hannibal levee waiting for their militia orders. A boat docked, a Union officer walked onto the levee, and "cordially offered the trio the option of accompanying him to St. Louis for enlistment as Union pilots, or being clapped into irons."[4] These Union officers got distracted—supposedly by some pretty girls—and Clemens and his pals ran for the country-side, where they managed to enroll in their militia. The truth of this tale is also questionable.

Throughout Missouri, there were complex feelings about taking sides. Three times as many Missouri men went to fight for the North as for the South. Clemens's home guard was against the Federal takeover. Sam came armed with his squirrel rifle, and rode a squat mule named Paint Brush. All were totally untrained, and almost shot each other during nighttime maneuvers.

If groups like Clemens's supported the Confederacy, they would likely get imprisoned or killed. If they supported the Union, they might win but would still lose their property and their slaves. Many men like Sam saw that a civil war may have had some just cause, but would end up with strangers killing strangers, all from the same nation, who in other times would have simply found another way to settle their differences.

After two months of undisciplined wandering, Sam Clemens got a chance to start his life over. His brother Orion had been awarded by President Abraham Lincoln the position of secretary to the governor of the Nevada Territory. Only Sam had enough money to pay for the trip, so Orion had to take him along as his aide. Also, Orion knew that Sam was trying to escape the Missouri state guard. Since the Clemens family had lost two sons, a daughter, and a father, Orion must have decided to at least try to save Sam.

It is worth noting that most people assumed the War Between the States would be brief. Sam himself relates some of his own feelings in "The Private History of a Campaign that Failed" in 1885.[5] Sam explains his own attitude by saying, "Thousands entered the war, got just a taste of it, and then stepped out again, permanently."[6] This is pretty much what he did. The following story has been judged to be both truth and fiction: When Sam's militia captain Lyman started to plan an assault, Sam realized, "Here was no jest. We were face to face with actual war...there was no hesitation, no indecision: we said that if Lyman wanted to meddle with these soldiers he could go ahead and do it; but if he waited for us to follow him, he would wait a long time."[7] Once in the midst of an enemy

A battle between Civil War gunboats being fought on the Mississippi in 1862. To avoid being forced to pilot such boats, Sam Clemens headed west.

raid, Sam claims he shot a man, who was not even the enemy. True or not, we are fortunate that Sam Clemens looked back from a distance. His "memoir" helps us never to try to settle things through combat again.

Life on the Mississippi

Mark Twain tirelessly inventories his life to service his fiction (especially when the fiction was presented as nonfiction).
—Historian Forrest Robinson[8]

Throughout his years in shipping Sam Clemens talked about writing a full work on his life on and love for the Mississippi River, and he compiled stories from 1863 to 1883, when he finally started to write the book. During those twenty years he thought up a lot to say. His book ended up being over six hundred pages plus appendices and 316 pen-and-ink illustrations! He must have figured that America's Big River deserved a Big Book.

Clemens started publishing parts of this book in the 1870s. Scholar Lawrence Howe tells us that he published seven "Sketches" in the *Atlantic Monthly* from January to August 1875 under the title "Old Times on the Mississippi."[9] Periodicals across the country liked these sketches so much that they pirated them—more proof to Clemens that the reading public was fascinated with the river. Later, he added to his observations secondary material from his vast readings on the river to make the complete six hundred-page book.

This Book's Content Covers It All

What was *Life on the Mississippi* really about? In the sixty chapter titles of this book, Clemens shows us that if a reader wants to find out anything at all about life on the river in the years before the Civil War, they can find it in his book. It is instructional, historical, geographical, social, biographical, and even humorous. He personally narrates it and claims it is nonfiction (it is considered a memoir), but we can sometimes wonder when both poetry and humor seem to take over a chapter.

One of the most moving chapters reinforces how much boys like Sam admired the possibility of traveling on the river. "The great Mississippi, the majestic, the magnificent Mississippi, rolling its mile-wide tide along, shining in the sun."[10] He depicts the quiet boredom pervading his small town until someone cries out, "Steamboat a-comin'!" Clemens then describes that "all in a twinkling the dead town is alive and moving."[11] He follows with a gorgeous description of the boat itself and the exciting transfer of crew, passengers, and freight, all within a matter of minutes. Then the boat sends out steam, breaks the river silence with loud whistles, sails on, and "the town is dead again."[12]

---

memoir

A true story that a person tells about his or her own life.

When he was young, Sam had many examples of how to join the world of steamboating from other Hannibal boys. They became "engineers," "mud clerks," barkeeps, and at the top of the heap, pilots. If they could do it, Sam dreamed, someday he could too.

In truth, Sam said, most Hannibal boys never left town, not even to see the great city upriver named St. Louis. Sam became the exception by going to cities in Iowa, Missouri, and Ohio as a journeyman printer. But he did not ride the river until he found sixteen dollars to book a passage from Cincinnati to New Orleans on "an ancient tub called the Paul

THE GOLDEN AGE OF STEAMBOATS

Robert Fulton invented the steam engine and built the first steamboat in 1807. The vessels soon sailed the 3,860 miles (6,212 kilometers) of the Mississippi, as well as other great American rivers. These boats were wide, stable, and could sail in shallow draft. By the 1830s, about 1,200 steamboats moved the produce and people of the Midwest, joining the Southern states with the rest of the Union. They also provided entertainment in the form of theater and gambling.

Jones."[13] As he sailed the Ohio River, he recalled the thrill. "I was a traveller! A word never had tasted so good in my mouth before."[14]

In *Life on the Mississippi*, young Sam's personal passion for this first step in his new life is contagious. The way he describes his jobs—the older crew bellowing their orders using their own brand of bullying and swearing ("I wished I could talk like that!" confessed Sam)—brings the reader right on board. We read chapters like these because they do what great narratives do: they put us smack-dab in the middle of the experience. And where did Sam start learning this kind of narrative? He claims from characters like the watchman from his first ship, whose narratives were "so reeking with bloodshed and so crammed with hair breadth escapes and the most engaging personal villainies [sic] that I sat speechless, enjoying, shuddering, wondering, worshipping."[15]

Sam later confesses that this watchman was hardly a heroic character; he was low, vulgar, and ignorant. But how he could spin a tale! And that must be the same reason we read *Life on the Mississippi*.

Natural Joys and Beauties: Why Sam Learned to Read and Love the River

Most people never think much about a river except as water they must get across on a bridge. A few lucky people may own a pleasure boat, take it out to fish, or drive past a river near their home. For Sam Clemens, the river was life's greatest mystery, to be revealed to him day by day.

> The face of the water became a wonderful book—which told its mind to me without reserve, delivering its most cherished secrets as clearly as if it uttered them with a voice...There was never so wonderful a book written by man, never one whose interest was so absorbing, so unflagging, so sparklingly renewed with every re-pe-rusal.[16]

When he was young and still learning every one of those cherished secrets, he had the liberty of absorbing the 1,200 miles (1,931 km) of natural beauty from St. Louis to New Orleans.

> I stood like one bewitched. I drank it in, in speechless rapture...But the day came when I began to cease from noting the glories and the charms which the moon and the sun and the twilight wrought upon the river's face.[17]

As a dedicated pilot, Sam had to stop being the poet-writer and start being the serious observer. Every switch or ripple in the current, or movement, or floating log, or wind change, meant something that determined how the boat needed to be steered. So as time passed and Sam matured, he started doing what he would do the rest of his life as an author: fall deeply into an experience, store it, and then later carefully use it for his craft and career.

Young Sam Clemens, about age twenty-five. He had not yet grown his signature mustache.

Life on the Mississippi does tend to ramble. Like the river itself, it takes its own time, stops to gossip, or plows slowly through a storm. Sam moves on from his piloting days, speaks of the Civil War, and tells tales about migrating freed blacks and other social issues taking place in the 1870s. Like the river itself, the book winds and seems to double back. The reader has to pay attention. But every character, scene, and resolution is worth the effort.

The later part of the book covers a trip Clemens made to revisit the river and its towns. He writes about a terrible flood in 1882 that showed how much damage the great river can do to those who live beside it. Chapter thirty-two jumps ahead to Sam Clemens spending time in Munich, Bavaria (Germany), and tells a bizarre tale. What does one have to do with the other? Often Clemens includes things for contrast, such as the startling modernization he found on his return to New Orleans in 1882, including the glare of electric lights and the convenience of an ice factory. All good travel books show change, for better or worse. No matter where this book may take the reader, one always returns—as did Sam Clemens—to the Big River itself.

Inspiration Comes From the West as Sam Clemens Becomes Mark Twain

Soon after Sam and Orion Clemens arrived in Carson City, Nevada, they realized that Orion would take over a lot of jobs as federal secretary, since the governor seemed to do little of the hard work of governing. Still, Orion could not find much for Sam to do as his aide.

To keep busy, Sam investigated how men were making money in Nevada and nearby northern California. He wrote back to his mother, Jane, that the land was "fabulously rich in gold, silver, copper, lead, coal, iron, quicksilver, marble, granite, chalk...gypsum," but admitted to her that he was told there was also an abundance of "thieves, murderers, desperadoes, ladies, children, lawyers, Christians, Indians, Chinamen, Spaniards, gamblers, sharpers...poets, preachers, and jackass rabbits."[1]

Mining was grueling work, but Sam still bought mining ground. He also found three partners: a friend from Keokuk, an old blacksmith, and a lawyer from Maine. These uninformed men never realized how easily one could get cheated. After a while, the quartet had "amassed more that thirty thousand feet apiece in 'mines' that essentially did not exist."[2]

Sam had a good time with the western characters he found in bars. He adopted their dress, wearing cowboy pants, boots, flannel shirts, and a big slouch hat. He grew a large moustache which would become his trademark look. These prospectors spun stories, drank whisky, and all believed their investments would somehow pay off. During the spring of 1862, Sam could see his debts rising and hopes falling. By June he was desperate, but said to Orion, "My back is sore, and my hands are blistered [from his pick and shovel], but something must come, you know."[3]

But nothing came. Historian Forrest Robinson summed it up: "Along with many others, he tried his hand at prospecting, and failed; he made timber claims, and failed; he speculated in mining stocks, and failed. [Sadly, his record here was starting

The desk where Sam Clemens worked as a reporter at the *Territorial Enterprise* in Virginia City, Nevada. He was soon to adopt his pen name.

to sound like that of his grandfather and father.] What didn't fail him was his pen."[4]

Perhaps Orion begged the editor of the Virginia City, Nevada, *Territorial Enterprise* to give his brother Sam a job. Because in September 1862, Samuel Clemens finally gave up his disastrous get-rich-quick schemes and began doing what he was meant to do with his life: write. He took a job as a full-time reporter for twenty-five dollars a week.[5]

Even without meaning to at the time, Sam stored his rambunctious adventures as a wild miner and speculator in his memory. He knew that along with reporting the news, he would try for a chance to sell short pieces to area newspapers, even send some brimming with western tales and adventures to newspapers back East. Although he probably did not know how much serious work full-time writing was, he learned to get over his tendency to be distracted and even lazy. When people recognized his natural skill, he showed how energetic he could be to impress them.

The young reporters at the *Territorial Enterprise* found that turning news into tall tales got them more readers and was a lot more fun to write. Sam reasoned that anyone could report what was plain to see. So he along with the others made up details that never happened! Their stories even included hoaxes—and added to a growing literary field known as frontier humor.

By the end of 1863, Sam Clemens was publishing his news stories and tall tales around the West. His friends told him he needed a catchy "pen name." Here the truth gets lost in myth. Some historians say it is obvious that the name "Mark Twain" came from his days as a river boat pilot—pole-men called a twelve-foot (three-meter) measurement, which was a safe depth, a mark twain. Others say the name was decided in a Nevada bar—where the term "mark twain" was used to say "two drinks marked on credit"—now time to pay up! Clemens enjoyed the coincidence and had heard the term on both occasions—perhaps it does not matter the reason he chose it as his pen name. It stuck, and gave Sam Clemens some protection from the folks he might ridicule or parody.

California, Here He Comes!

In 1864, Twain grew famous enough to secure work with San Francisco newspapers. He wrote for the San Francisco *Morning Call*, a daily newspaper, and also for two literary magazines. Unfortunately Twain felt he had to tell the truth as a big city reporter and got into trouble for criticizing the city police department. The story get even weirder when a rival reporter upbraided Twain and challenged him to a duel![6] Since dueling had not been legal since 1861, and Twain was a poor shot, he decided to do the sensible thing: retreat.

Twain hid out in the Sierra Foothills at a cabin on Jackass Hill and started writing. One of his stories from that period became his first unexpected claim for national attention.

"Jim Smiley and His Jumping Frog"

The story was originally given this title when Mark Twain published it in the New York *Saturday Press* in November 1865. The tale was an instant hit and quickly got picked up by other periodicals. "The Celebrated Jumping Frog of Calaveras County" was the second title Twain used, as the story was revised and republished in December 1865.

Short, silly, and delightful, the "Jumping Frog" shows the passion for tall tales and folk humor that had taken over the West. The tale is framed by a first person narrator (Mark Twain himself) who is in search of anyone who can locate a friend's friend, an old man named Leonidas Smiley. A miner named Simon Wheeler does not know Leonidas Smiley; he knows *Jim* Smiley. Before the narrator can leave, he is caught up in the tale of Jim Smiley, a man who would bet on anything.

One example of Jim's addictive betting concerns racing his mare.

> He used to win money on that horse for all she was so slow and always had the asthma or the distemper, or the consumption...they used to give her two or three hundred yards start and then pass her underway. But always at the fag-end of the race she'd get excited and desperate-like and come cavorting and spraddling up, and scattering her legs around sometimes in the air, sometimes out to one side...kicking up more dust, and raising more racket with her coughing and sneezing and blowing her nose, and always fetch up at the stand just about a neck ahead![7]

After betting on horse races and dog fights and every other competition, Jim invents a new way to gamble: frog racing! The plot rolls along as Jim trains a large frog named Dan'l Webster to jump on command. As he tells gullible friends, "He can out-jump any frog in Calaveras county."[8]

Amazingly, Twain keeps the reader enthralled with the success of this jumping frog and the way he and his gambling master are brought down. As with all tall tales, this one ends with the narrator trying to get away before Simon Wheeler (who really knows nothing about Leonidas) sucks him into hearing another crazy story. The reader is, of course, dying to hear the story that Twain leaves untold. The great success of this tale gave Twain the drive to compile a whole collection of short stories from magazines, newspapers, and his own store. Called *The Celebrated Jumping Frog of Calaveras County and*

A caricature of Twain on a frog refers to his story "The Celebrated Jumping Frog of Calaveras County." Notice: the Twain mustache has arrived.

Other Sketches. This was published in 1867; it was his very first book.

Roughing It

As usual, Mark Twain took years to turn certain life experiences into literary material. He was married and living in Buffalo, New York, in 1871 when he wrote *Roughing It*. By this time, he had written some other books that covered his experiences traveling in America and abroad. None of those experiences, however, seemed as amazing and downright funny as those he had in the Nevada Territory and Northern California when he was a beginning prospector, reporter, and writer in the early 1860s.

After much struggle and research, Twain's memory got rolling, producing a book of 580 pages. If the reader is daunted by so much material, he can simply check the table of contents, where each of the seventy-nine chapters has a detailed heading covering each and every subject. Twain followed this same style, common in nineteenth century fiction, in *Life on the Mississippi*. Readers can find such headings as "Between a Wink and an Earthquake," "Slumgullion," "Bemis finds refuge in a tree," "A Warm but too familiar a Bedfellow," and other intriguing subjects. Twain later claimed that his favorite chapter was the eighth, in which he chronicles the long and dangerous work of the Pony Express riders. All these subjects were fascinating to readers in the East.

Twain Weaves Humor and Satire into Travel Reporting

Some chapters in *Roughing It* are worth reading as a group, for they follow a particular subject in Twain's western experiences. Chapters twelve through sixteen, for example, focus on his attempts to understand the history and beliefs of the Mormons, or the Church of Jesus Christ of Latter-Day Saints. A bit later, chapter twenty-five covers "The Mormons in Nevada—how to persuade a loan from them." Although reporting on a controversial religion is a serious task, Twain cannot resist many sly moments of satire.

In these chapters Twain talks about meeting several Mormons while traveling. He was heading west by stagecoach, for the railroad had not yet been laid. He describes overtaking a group of Mormon emigrants traveling in thirty-three wagons:

> Tramping wearily along and driving their herd of loose cows were dozens of coarse-clad and sad-looking men, women and children who had walked as they were walking now...for eight lingering weeks, and in that time had compassed the distance our stage had come in eight days and three hours—seven hundred and ninety-eight miles! They were dusty, uncombed, hatless, ragged and they did look so tired![9]

Twain's coach was able to make such good time because they changed their six-mule team at stations every few hours, "and did it nearly every time in four minutes."[10] He does not tell us how often the passengers were allowed to eat, drink, or sleep, but does mention that one stop included a bath in a creek—a delight because "it was very seldom our furious coach halted long enough for an indulgence of that kind!"[11]

As they passed through the Rockies, the coach driver gestured to Soda Lake, a dry bed where the Mormons traveled down from Great Salt Lake City, their religious center. He said they shoveled up wagons of "saleratus" which is sodium bicarbonate, the ingredient used in baking powder. Then they drove it back to Salt Lake City where "they could sell it for twenty-five cents a pound."[12] This level of labor and ingenuity impressed Twain.

The stagecoach trail included a stop called South Pass City, where "the hotel keeper, the blacksmith, the mayor, the constable, the city marshal and the principal citizen…all came out to greet us cheerily…and we gave him good day."[13] The city consisted of ten citizens, and Twain was moved to observe that if one of the job holders died, "the people might stand it; but if he were to die all over, it would be a frightful loss to the community."[14]

His impressions of the Latter Day Saints in Salt Lake City are vivid and often seem to stretch the truth. He is of course interested in polygamy, which was practiced extensively and legally at that time. He also reports on Mormon drinking practices, which are limited to something called Valley Tan—"a kind of whiskey or first cousin to it, of Mormon invention and manufactured only in Utah. Tradition says it is made of fire and brimstone."[15] No public drinking was allowed, and privately, only this Valley Tan was permitted, says Twain, with a wink of his eye.

He then reports on the supposed healthy lifestyle of Salt Lake City. "They declared there was only one physician in the place, and he was arrested every week regularly and held to answer under the vagrancy act for having 'no visible means of support.'"[16]

As for the practice of one husband for many wives, Twain says he was opposed, until he saw the Mormon women. Alas, he found them "poor, ungainly, pathetically 'homely' creatures." His only conclusion is that, as he tears up, "the man that marries one of them has done an act of Christian charity which entitles him to the kindly applause of mankind, not censure." He then goes even further by proclaiming that the man who marries sixty of them should be regarded as a national hero![17] Here we see Twain do a turnabout, when he hears testimony revealing what the household of Brigham Young, his many wives, and fifty-odd children is really like. He can't resist a four-page rant in the supposed voice of Brigham Young about the wildly jealous, possessive relationships between his many wives and offspring, most of which he can only recall by a number and not by a name. Twain is learning that he can be quite funny, but must always take care not to go over the top. And when he attempts to give the reader his take on the details of the Book of Mormon and the precepts of the religion, it is definitely time for the lapsed Presbyterian to step back and move on.

Political Correctness Goes Out the Window

The reader might stop here to check Twain's Prefatory at the start of the book. This letter tells, in his already quirky, satirical voice, how Twain plans to write this personal narrative. His goal is to help the reader "while away an idle hour"—not pressure him with metaphysics or science. He then admits "there is a good deal of information in the book. I regret this very much…information appears to stew out of me naturally."[18]

This claim is only partly true, for when Twain backtracks from Salt Lake City some 200 miles (321 km), his information gets questionable. He says he comes upon a tribe he calls the Goshoot Indians. "I have been obliged to look the bulky volumes of Wood's 'Uncivilized Races of Men' clear through to find a savage tribe degraded enough to rank with the Goshoots."[19] He describes them as scrawny, sneaking, and treacherous looking, with skin "a dull black like the ordinary American Negro." He can't stop here, claiming the Goshoots must have descended from a gorilla, or kangaroo, or Norway rat. This "information" is clearly not accurate.

And it gets worse, for Twain (who we do not think had any extensive personal relations with actual Indians in the time he spent in Nevada and California) says that if a person were to take away the romance given to Indians by writers like James Fenimore Cooper (whom he disliked), he will be disgusted. The Indian remains "filthy, treacherous, and repulsive."[20] This attack comes from a man who admits he had only one bath on a nearly nine-week sweaty stagecoach trip. Critics have always been confused about who the Goshoots represented and why Twain thought that including them in his account was darkly comic.

Twain continues in *Roughing It* to cover his years as a struggling silver miner, rambling prospector, and small-town newspaper reporter. Every interesting character he can recall pops up in his chapters. He includes all kinds of excitement, such as earthquakes and explosions. He also satirizes the fraud committed by second-rate politicians running the state governments, something he learned well from his brother Orion.

The *San Francisco Examiner* had sent Twain on a fact-finding journey to the Sandwich Islands (in Hawaii) in 1866. He wrote down many impressions and interviews, so he retrieved this journal and revised some of his most interesting observations to be included in this book. People knew little of Hawaii in the mid-nineteenth century. Twain recalled enough to fill chapters sixty-two through seventy-eight in *Roughing It*. Twain does not spare readers the savage attack led by King Kamehameha of Honolulu, whom he considered a military genius. This king took over the island of Oahu, then impaled the heads of the former king and his chiefs on spikes. Such things did happen in early Hawaiian history.

But the Goshoots and the anti-Indian rant? There was little truth in Twain's words. But critics of the time enjoyed the far-out humor so much that they never seemed to care. In the 1870s, the United States Cavalry was at war with several Native American tribes most of the time, so bias against the tribes was common. As for Twain, he lived the rest of his life seemingly without spending any time with Indians and never looked back at the grossly bigoted portrait he had painted.

Roughing It came out to a pre-sale subscription list of over thirty thousand fans eager to see if they liked it as well as *The Innocents Abroad*, Twain's travel memoir of 1869. They certainly did. Biographer Ron Powers reports that by the end of 1872, *Roughing It* brought in $22,000 for its author in American sales alone[21]—a sizable sum in the 1870s.

West Coast critics thought this book was hilarious. Critics from Boston, Hartford, and New York also enjoyed the book, especially its descriptions of the Wild West. They picked up on the book's style of exaggeration and broad irony, the use of the author as the narrator with all his faults and fancies, and its creation of new tall tales to expand this American literary form. Critics were pleased that the book did not spare the blunt, vulgar language of the Westerners, yet made them completely genuine and appealing. All, of course, except the Goshoots, who never got to say a word, since apparently they did not exist. Also, no reviews came in from the Mormons, who we hope at that time—as today—relied on their sense of humor.

irony

Language whose meaning is the opposite of what the speaker actually intends.

Olivia "Livy" Langdon at the time she fell in love with Sam Clemens

Family Life

In February 1870, Mark Twain married the beautiful, petite Olivia Langdon, whom he called Livy. She agreed to marry him after he had written her "an estimated 189 love letters."[22] By March 1872, they had a one-year-old son, Langdon. The boy had a difficult infancy, and at this age could still not sit up alone, nor imitate sounds, and cried frequently.

In 1871 the Clemens family moved as renters into Hartford, Connecticut's pleasant Nook Farm neighborhood. In 1874 they built a massive brick home at 351 Farmington Avenue. The couple had expensive tastes, and builders and decorators took advantage of this. Yet the house turned out to be a magnificent example of the period's architecture and style. Twain's humble childhood and rambling bachelor years all across the West made having this special place for Livy and his children a dream come true. He exclaimed, "It is a home—& the word never had so much meaning before."[23]

During the 1870s, Twain was making a lot of his living touring the country as a humorous lecturer. One might say he was inventing what we now call standup comedy. Sometimes critics razzed him, made fun of his rambling gait, drawling speech, and carrot-colored hair. Yet his audiences were huge, and each evening ended with them dissolved in laughter. Twain could have kept this up for a long time, but he and Livy missed each other terribly. It was time to return to his home in Hartford, where he had his family, his library, a quiet office, writing desk, books, cigars, and his billiard table. He was ready to write more great books.

From Tall Tales to Olde Legends: Twain Moves to the Sixteenth Century

By the time Mark Twain published his next major work, he had a new audience at home. The dedication in this book says, "To Those good-mannered and agreeable children SUSIE AND CLARA CLEMENS. This book is affectionately inscribed by their father."[1]

Although Sam and Livy had lost their son, Langdon, to diphtheria (an acute bacterial disease which sends a toxin through the blood, causing fatal heart and nerve damage), they had two bright, healthy daughters. Susan was born in March 1872, and Clara in June 1874. Their father never got over his grief from losing Langdon, and even blamed himself for taking the little boy out in cold weather for a stroll. Of course, he was wrong to feel guilty. Diphtheria could be contracted at any time, and there was no vaccine or medicine to cure it.

Susie and Clara had literate parents who read to them continually, creating a hunger for stories from their dad every evening. In later life the girls recalled that these stories covered a wide variety of fantasies and history. Twain apparently did not record them in writing. We do know that he always loved medieval British literature, particularly the legends of Robin Hood. He had taught his less literate pals in Hannibal about the cruel monarchs, tough punishments for the slightest crime, and the need for a defender of the poor. The woods around Hannibal substituted for Sherwood Forest, as the boys acted out the stories of their hero. In 1880 Twain researched and wrote an adult story called "1601 or Conversation as it was by the social fireside in the time of the Tudors." His interest in this period may have resulted in his next popular book, *The Prince and the Pauper*.

The Prince and the Pauper: The Mostly True Legend of Edward VI of England

In the early 1880s, Mark Twain received many fan letters telling him that both younger and older readers were enjoying

The Clemens family (*from left*), Clara, Olivia, Jean, Sam, and Susy, enjoying their pet dog

his books. He had definitely perfected the "crossover novel." Readers wanted him to write more about Tom Sawyer and Huck Finn, as well as more exciting adventure stories like *Roughing It*. Twain knew that his readers and his children would enjoy that kind of adventure, but he decided he would set his latest story in medieval England. After a trip to London got him fired up, Twain began reading British history. There he discovered the perfect little hero: Prince Edward VI of England, son of King Henry VIII, who became King of England.

Although the sixteenth century was a long time ago, Twain found many writings of the period on the ways of the British monarchy, social class discrimination, the laws and punishments, and the true life of Prince Edward. Twain took a lesson from one of his favorite authors, playwright William Shakespeare, who also "brushed up" on ancient historic tales and legends and then used them in his immortal dramas.

So how much "truth" did Twain find and use? Since he knew everyone would ask, he put his explanation up front in *The Prince and the Pauper*'s preface:

> I will set down a tale as it was told to me by one who had it of his father...and so on, back and still back, three hundred years and more, the fathers transmitting it to the sons and so preserving it. It may be history, it may be only legend, a tradition. It may have happened, it may not have happened, but it could have happened. It may be that the wise and the learned believed it in the old days; it may be that only the unlearned and the simple loved it and credited it. —The Author.[2]

The "truth" about Edward VI is short and simple and sad. He was the only son of King Henry VIII. This famous king had a daughter with Queen Catherine of Aragon, another daughter with Queen Anne Boleyn, and finally this baby boy with Queen Jane Seymour. These queens had no luck: Catherine got divorced, Anne got executed, and Jane caught the post-birth infection called child-bed fever, and promptly died. But their children—Mary, Elizabeth, and Edward—survived to adulthood.

Motherless Edward was raised by ladies of the king's household, nannies, and relatives of his birth mother, Jane Seymour. His stepsister Elizabeth, four years older, was very fond of him. Finally King Henry wed his seventh wife, Catherine Parr. This good queen saw the need to educate the bright young prince, but not to isolate him from other children. She set up a palace school full of tutors, plus children of well-born courtiers to learn and play with him. Edward excelled in academics, languages, royal duties, riding, music, even fencing. His favorite pal was a boy named Barnaby Fitzpatrick who also got the job of, yes, the Royal Whipping Boy. He took Edward's punishments when he failed in his lessons. It is written that although Edward was gifted intellectually, he had temper fits, and the Whipping Boy took his spankings for that.[3]

Edward VI was almost ten years old when his father died. The rule in Britain was that the male heir took the throne, no matter how young. So Edward was crowned in 1547. Heartbroken over his father's death and fearful about how he might be used in palace politics, the boy tried hard to see which of his advisers he could trust. Not only was he a perceptive boy, but he believed he was destined to rule. He kept up his demanding studies, and began to sit in on council meetings regarding laws of the country. Soon he understood many adult problems, like Britain's military situation, and the establishment of a Prot-

King Edward VI of England, the true subject of Twain's fictional book *The Prince and the Pauper*

estant church as the country's official religion. King Edward started to make his will known to the elder royals.

One thing King Edward VI was ignorant about was the sorry lives of most of his subjects. It was likely that he was protected from greeting them to keep him from catching diseases. It is said he made one ruling: he was against burning heretics alive (heretics were people against the Christian Church of England). This shows that Edward was beginning to realize that hideous brutal punishments should be eliminated.

It is hard to believe, given Edward's high level of care and feeding, but he did get sick. He contracted tuberculosis, a lung disease which comes from inhaling the bacteria of an infected person or animal. At this time there was no cure nor medication to save the patient. This gifted young king died in 1553. He was just seventeen.[4]

Two Boys—Two Worlds—Danger in Each!

Mark Twain knew that every great adventure story needs a serious conflict. But where was the conflict in Edward's story? How much mischief could this boy-prince-turned-king find? The real Edward was uppity and spoiled, but he was also highly intelligent and dedicated to ruling his nation. Twain must have thought of the classic story that went back to Roman times: mistaken identity of two people who look enough alike to be twins. Then he decided he would not only tell the tale of a prince, but also that of a pauper. So he invented the fictional character of Tom Canty. Edward and Tom could show us the entire breadth of British society: the untouchable royals on top, and the brutal and brutalized poor on the bottom. The scary struggles of both boys to survive in each others' world made for the conflict!

The plot of *The Prince and the Pauper* is complex and at times unbelievable. Prince Edward and Tom Canty, boys born on the same day who bear an amazing resemblance to each other, meet by a fluke. Tom is taken into the palace by the Prince, where they do a boyish thing: they try on each other's outfits. The Prince asks Tom a little about his family life, and is shocked to hear that he is beaten and forced to beg and steal. Soon guards mistake Edward for Tom and toss him out into the busy London streets, where he is swept away by the low element of Tom's world. Tom is assumed to be the Prince and is taken into the royal world with all its ceremonies and deviousness. When both boys protest that they are the other, it is assumed they have gone slightly mad.

After this, Edward is faced with difficult situations and barely survives physically and emotionally. Tom Canty conquers his panic about being punished for impersonating the prince. Having been taught by a priest in his early boyhood to read and understand some Latin, he succeeds at passing himself off as Edward. However, guilt eats at him as he thinks of the danger the real Edward faces. The boys survive near misses, and when King Henry VIII dies and the true Edward must ascend the throne, they both know it is now or never. Once Tom Canty is crowned king, Prince Edward will be doomed. Twain keeps readers gasping as the boys work their way through villains, guards, and mob scenes, and finally touch hands at the last moment of the coronation.

Themes and Social Attitudes Fill the Book

This novel is rich in themes and moral lessons for readers of all ages. The upper class held all the power in the 1500s. America's own mid-nineteenth-century interests were still controlled

The cover of *The Prince and the Pauper,* edition published in 1882. (The first edition came out in 1881.)

by the wealthy. Twain criticizes and satirizes both centuries by covering the following themes.

The strict class structure of British society and the desperate situation of the poor are a major theme. From the mid-sixteenth to the mid-nineteenth century, lack of education and opportunity remained the same for the lower class. Twain knew that conditions in the slums of American cities in his day were abysmal. He wants his readers to look back and see where it began.

The strength and determination of two ten-year-old boys who refuse to give up makes for a gripping story. Twain takes some of the flavor of Tom Sawyer and his pals—who lived safe, comfortable lives compared to Tom Canty—and celebrates these boys's spirits of endurance, bravado, grit, and independence. The young were powerless in the sixteenth century, yet Tom and Edward, with the help of a few good adults, make it through.

theme
A distinctive quality or concern in one or more works of fiction.

The ridicule of superstition was common and cruel and did little good. Every society seems to have had its superstitions. Twain confesses to his own in *Tom Sawyer*. In this book, he addresses the dark side and the foolishness of people's unfounded beliefs. Witchery proves quite dangerous for the innocents. During a time in prison, Edward is forced to watch two accused women who were kind to him be burned at the stake with their children beside them. He bemoans that such should happen "in England! Ay, there's the shame of it—not in Heathenesse, but Christian England!...and I, whom they have comforted, must look on and see the great wrong done."[5]

Mixed up "twins" and confused identities add to the suspenseful plot. This device, which advances the adventure, can create some humor as well. In this story the "twin" boys each have a lot of strong points in common. This shows the reader that whether a person is born as rich as a royal or as poor as a beggar, he has it in him to better himself and do right by others.

Unjust punishment by the penal system must be reformed. In centuries past, punishments were horrendous, even for petty crimes. Probably the most famous case of this was celebrated by Victor Hugo in his 1862 novel *Les Misérables*. Twain wants his nineteenth-century readers to wake up and consider prison reform. He states that in the British penal code during his day, 238 crimes were still punishable by execution. He underlines how bad things were in chapter twenty-seven, when Edward VI shouts to a poor branded prisoner, "Within a month thou shalt be free; and the laws that have dishonoured thee, and shamed the English name shall be swept from the statute books...kings should go to school to their own laws at times, and so learn mercy."[6]

The parody of the band of vagabond thieves that kidnap Prince Edward shows most criminals are really no good! These crooks are so far from Robin Hood and his Merry Men that they steal from the poor and give to themselves. Twain may want us to consider the prevalence of highway robbery during his time, and ask ourselves: what would Robin Hood think if he showed up today?

The imagery of Prince Edward as Christ-like may not be purposeful, but readers should look for these references and decide. For example: Edward, dressed as humble Tom the beggar, is shoved and ridiculed for saying that he is the king.[7] When Edward is lost and cold, he is sheltered in a stable by the animals and their straw, where their warmth saves him.[8] When two young girls believe in him, Edward says, "When I am come to mine own again, I will always honor little children, remembering how they trusted me and believed in me in my time of trouble."[9] Twain wants his readers to understand that there are many layers beneath a person's exterior, and it matters little how they are dressed or speak.

Life in the Extreme: Why Were Both Boys Unhappy?

Living as another boy in very different circumstances brings great stress and unhappiness. One might think that after an amount of time has passed, Tom Canty would begin to revel in the treatment given him as prince. But his character is such that he dislikes the role. As a boy of the streets, he was often in danger, but he was free. He had no social rules, no expectations. As Prince Edward, Tom Canty is trapped by the continual foolish details of royal life. "He was cordially glad when the ceremony was ended. The larger part of his day was 'wasted'—as he termed it in his own mind—in labors pertaining to his royal office. Even the two hours devoted to certain princely pastimes and recreations were a burden to him...they were so fettered by restrictions and ceremonious observances."[10]

> **imagery**
>
> Words that paint a picture, describing how something looks, feels, sounds, etc.

Finally, Tom's guilt at abandoning his real mother (who spots him in a procession and calls out to him) overcomes him. The honesty in him rises up, and as he exclaims, "Would to God I were free of my captivity!"[11]

Prince Edward also feels miserable being stuck in his hard, hungry, danger-filled existence. The amount of violence he witnesses may be realistic for the Middle Ages, but probably shocked young readers of the nineteenth century. Edward encounters a knight who has been wrongly cheated of his inheritance and through simple goodness tries to protect a "mad boy" who thinks he is a royal. Miles Hendon is a character of strength and honor, but one who has been deceived by his own clan. Twain wants us to realize that even those who have plenty in life will cheat others to have more, but will usually be found out in the end. Prince Edward greatly rewards Miles Hendon once he returns to his throne.

Although unhappy during his ordeal, Edward does grow and learn. The most shocking thing to readers today is to discover how completely ignorant Edward was kept about the way his subjects were forced to live. Being so sheltered, without our means of mass communication, he unknowingly allowed terrible injustices to take place. The underlying message for readers both young and old is a simple one: spend time in another person's life—or as the Native American saying goes, walk a mile in his moccasins—and you will become more just, compassionate, and even merciful.

To underscore this idea, Twain opens the book with a quote from Shakespeare (who used the mixed-up twins theme in his play *The Comedy of Errors*). "The quality of mercy is twice blessed; it blesseth him that gives, and him that takes; 'Tis mightiest in the mightiest; it becomes the throned monarch better than his crown." —*The Merchant of Venice*.

The Prince and the Pauper Finds its Audience

Twain spent the winter evenings of 1881, before the book was published, reading it aloud to his wife, daughters Susy and Clara (ages nine and seven), and a lady houseguest. Years later, Susy Clemens would state it was "unquestionably the best book he had ever written...the book is full of lovely, charming ideas. And oh the language! It is perfect."[12] Livy and their guest Mary Fairbanks praised it as well. Fairbanks said, "A lovely book...your masterpiece in fineness."[13] The book pleased critics, even though they missed Twain's usual amount of dark humor and biting satire. When it came out by Christmas 1881, a *Hartford Courant* critic wrote, "Mark Twain has finally fulfilled the earnest hope of many friends in writing a book which has other and higher merits than can possibly belong to the most artistic expression of mere humor."[14]

A very special fan, the Clemens's neighbor Harriet Beecher Stowe, also gave her review. Twain wrote in his *Notebooks* that the famous author took his hand and said, "I am reading your 'Prince & the Pauper' for the fourth time, & and I know it's the best book for young folk that was ever written."[15]

Mark Twain himself was delighted with the great public acceptance of *The Prince and the Pauper*. He wrote to a critic that "literarily, the new departure is a great deal better received that I had any right to hope for."[16]

Mark Twain Fails in Business but Wins in Literature

Mark Twain knew from the start that his wife, Olivia, would want to spend time each year with her family in Elmira, New York. In 1869 Twain lived all summer with the Langdon family, then married Livy in her family home the following winter. The Langdon's summer home, called Quarry Farm, was relaxing for Twain. It was in Elmira that Livy gave birth to Susan in 1872 and Clara in 1874, and finally Jean in 1880. The family provided Twain with a private study away from the house, so he had no excuses not to work. Livy, along with servants and family support, was able to care for her small children and still enjoy evenings with her husband.[1]

In his Quarry Farm study during the summer of 1876, Twain began working on a book he had long considered attempting. In letters to his brother Orion and sister-in-law Mollie, his mother Jane, and his friend W.D. Howells, Twain talked about tackling this project. "I began another boy's book...I have written 400 pages on it. It is Huck Finn's Autobiography. I like it only tolerably well, as far as I have got, and may possibly pigeonhole or burn the MS when it is done."[2]

We can see that Twain was facing some hard truths about this novel. It kept leading him down many paths. Huck's life was a struggle—a brutalized boy and a social outsider, to

Twain writes during the summer in his study at Quarry Farm, Elmira, New York.

whom only Tom Sawyer and possibly Miss Watson's slave Jim, meant anything. Where would Twain find fun and adventure with this young man? Moral issues kept cropping up in Twain's mind, the main one being the fact that a decade after the Civil War ended and slaves were emancipated, racial prejudice was as strong as ever in America. He had recently finished writing *The Gilded Age: Tale of Today* in 1873, and since this book dealt with the fraud that people perpetrated on each other, especially the lower economic class, this issue was still fresh to him as well.

Mark Twain did not burn Huckleberry Finn's autobiography. He buried it. Eight years later, spending the summer of 1883 in Elmira, he dug up his old manuscript, and began to write.

What Occupied Twain for Those Eight Years?

Mark Twain wrote smaller works. The expensive job of building his mansion in Hartford kept draining his bank account, so he had to work. These works included a stage play version of *The Gilded Age*, and a serial called "Old Times on the Mississippi" in the *Atlantic* magazine.

Twain wrote short fiction like "A True Story. Repeated word for word as I heard it" in 1874. This tale was told by the author about his "servant" Aunt Rachel. Rachel spoke only in her African American dialect, marking the first time Twain wrote in this style. Another story, "The White Elephant," a grown-up detective tale taking place in Siam (renamed Thailand in 1949), centered on the reverence held for the sacred white elephant which could be owned only by royalty. The story was not published until 1882. Twain did some traveling overseas in 1878 and 1879, taking his wife, children, and nanny along. This resulted in another travel book called *A Tramp Abroad* in 1880. All his work continued to sell well enough to keep up the Clemens family lifestyle. Almost. For 1882, biographer Ron Powers reports that the Clemens's domestic, business, and investment outlays were exceeding $100,000 for the year.[3] This comes to about $2 million in today's money. Although his writing and speaking income kept flowing, Mark Twain's investments were usually losers. It was time for another big book.

Twain Takes a River Refresher

In order to tell the tale of Huckleberry Finn, Twain needed to observe and listen to the paddle boats, the people, and the Mississippi River again. It had been twenty-one years since he worked the steamboat trade. When he arrived in Hannibal in 1882, he was almost too late, because the railroads had taken over most of the travel business. He saw that boys didn't want to pilot river boats as much as drive trains. The name of one surviving stern-wheeler that he spotted pleased him: it was called the *Mark Twain*.[4]

The small towns had grown, and the populations had blossomed. Yet their style of life and speech had not changed. Black people were emancipated, but lived as second-class citizens. Anti-black feeling was everywhere in the South. But the river itself, although it had flooded and done some damage, was still the Big Muddy he loved. He felt that the parts of *Huckleberry Finn* that he had roughed out years ago would still work.

When he returned East, Twain realized that he would be writing a book as big as the river. So he hired something new in the writers' world: a typist. Typewriters in the 1880s were slow and simple, and yet they were worlds beyond hand-copying, which is what authors had to do in the past. Corrections could more clearly be written on a typed page. Twain said, "My copying is always done on the type-writer now, and I shall not be likely to ever use any other system."[5] Of course, he first had to write the book!

Sam got back into the groove of Hannibal and the lower Mississippi in the 1840s. He poured out as much as four thousand words a day on *Huckleberry Finn*. It would be two more years until this challenging book was complete.

Major Changes from *Tom Sawyer* to *Huckleberry Finn*

The Adventures of Tom Sawyer is written from the third-person point of view. It makes use of the omniscient narrator, who tells us everything we need to know about everyone in the book. Yes, it is Tom's story, but we believe Mr. Twain the author as to what is true.

> **omniscient narrator**
>
> An all-knowing voice that tells the story and is able to know the thoughts of all of the characters.

The book includes the lives of Tom's Aunt Polly, half brother Sid, cousin Mary, and their friends, plus other residents of St. Petersburg. It introduces us to Huckleberry Finn, his nasty father Pap Finn, his girlfriend Becky, and some of Tom's best pals and enemies. Tom's passion for adventure and dangerous behaviors is seen throughout the book, and although Tom thinks he has the right to do these things, we can see that others in the story believe he is wrong, and deserves punishment.

Adventures of Huckleberry Finn was written differently. It is a first-person autobiography, or memoir. Huckleberry tells us his entire story as he lives it. This means the reader has to take Huck's word for whatever happens and why it does. However, this does not mean that Huck always represents Mark Twain's beliefs.

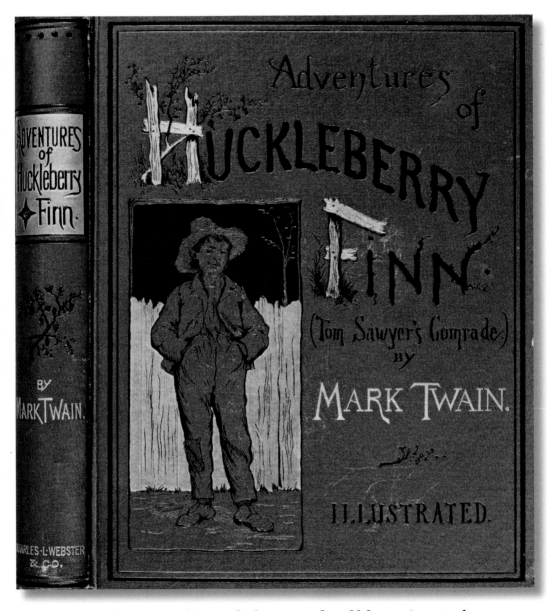

Cover of the first edition of *Adventures of Huckleberry Finn.* Huck is noted as Tom Sawyer's "comrade," as he stands before Tom's whitewashed fence.

---

first person

In the voice of "I," being told from one person's viewpoint.

What Mark Twain chose to do was probably a first in American fiction. He created an honest, simple youth living in slave-holding Missouri in the pre-Civil War period. He then used Huck to display all the assumptions about enslaved black people that any white boy would then have made. Even Huck, raised in the lowest class of white families, assumes that enslaved black people are items of property, inferior even to him. But Mark Twain, we believe, did not hold this assumption. So Huck, his first-person narrator, did not represent Twain the author. Huck is a reliable narrator—with unreliable beliefs.

This was complicated stuff for American fiction—and continued to cause a lot of trouble for this book for a century. Knowing this, we must take a close look at Huck's character, as well as the others who are part of his living adventure.

The Best Growing Up Story Ever

Huck Finn *is a monument that no puny pecking will destroy. It is built of indestructible blocks of human nature; if the blocks do not always fit, and the ornaments do not always agree, we need not fear. Time will blur the incongruities and moss over the mistakes. The edifice will grow more beautiful with the years."*

– Biographer Albert B. Paine[6]

Major Characters Join Our Hero

Huckleberry Finn is obviously the central character, but on the title page his name is followed by this description: "(Tom Sawyer's comrade). Scene: The Mississippi Valley. Time: forty to fifty years ago." This is an unusual way to begin a novel in the nineteenth century, but it ties us as readers to everything set down in the 1876 novel *The Adventures of Tom Sawyer*. Since this new book was published in 1885, it would be covering the years around 1840, a year after *Tom Sawyer* was set. Huck would be about thirteen or fourteen years old. Huck starts his memoir by referring to the story of his friend Tom, saying its author Mr. Mark Twain "told the truth, mainly. There were things that he stretched, but mainly he told the truth."[7]

What is the truth about Huck Finn? It is quite "a stretch" to believe that this boy almost raised himself. With no family but his useless father, who at the time of this book had been missing for a year, how does Huck survive on scraps, fishing, wearing rags and living in the wild, sleeping in what he calls his "sugar-hogshead," a large barrel? Children like young Sam Clemens had good parents, a warm house and decent food, and still died of diseases. Yet Huck is a tough kid who seems to thrive on garbage! None of the respectable boys are allowed to play with Huck. Tom Sawyer and his gang have to meet him secretly in their hideouts.

Huck has developed his wits and skills in order to stay alive. He does not cry about his life, he embraces it. When Huck is adopted by the Widow Douglas, he tells us right off "it was rough living in the house, considering how dismal regular and decent the widow was in all her ways."[8] He would run away, if not for a deal he made with Tom Sawyer that if he stayed, he could remain a member in their imaginary Robber Gang.

The Widow Douglas and Miss Watson

These good-hearted women believe it is their Christian duty to teach Huck reading, writing, and the Bible. The only "education" Huck seems to have is extensive knowledge of folklore and superstition, which as Christians they distrust.

The ladies include lessons in social behavior, which are mainly wasted. Widow Douglas and Miss Watson own slaves, whom they insist must say evening prayers with them. As Southern American Christians, they do not question the morality of owning people as property. Here is where their Christianity becomes confusing.

Jim

Jim may be one of the first major black characters in American fiction since Harriet Beecher Stowe's Uncle Tom in *Uncle Tom's Cabin*. Slaves in Stowe's novels, written before the Civil War, were so sympathetic that they moved thousands of Americans to support abolition of slavery. Jim is a more realistic model of the black men Twain knew from his family slaves. Honest and hard working, he speaks in a humble black dialect. Raised without any education other than superstition and folklore (much like Huck Finn), Jim "was more looked up to than any other nigger in that country."[9] He is a self-styled expert on witches and spells, and owns a powerful talisman. His character is driven by the dream of gaining freedom so he can earn enough to buy his own wife and two children out of slavery. Jim also has his own sense of personal conscience, of right and wrong, which he explains to Huck throughout the story.[10]

Pap Finn

Huckleberry's father reappears after being missing for over a year. He sneaks into the Widow's house and is in such terrible shape from alcoholism and malnutrition that Huck believes he need not fear him anymore. This proves to be a mistake. The elder Finn may be pasty and worn, but he is still evil to the core. Furious that Huck has now learned to read—which no other Finn ever managed to do—he roars, "You stop putting on frills. If I catch you about that school, I'll tan you good. First you know, you'll get religion too."[11] Not above kidnapping his own son and beating him until he was "all over welts" from a hickory switch, Pap Finn is the kind of lowlife that today we would call a career petty criminal and child abuser. Villains were common in nineteenth century novels, but few were as loathsome as Pap Finn.

Judge Thatcher

The Judge is Becky Thatcher's father, a good character from *Tom Sawyer*, who tries to protect Huck and his finances.

The Grangerfords and the Shepherdsons

These two farm families who live in southern Missouri exemplify the kind of decent people who get themselves into stupid feuds until the guns come out and people get killed. These families give Huck somewhere to hide from those who pursue him and Jim.

The Duke and the Dauphin

These two crooks (we don't learn their true names) may be the most tiresome characters in all of Twain's books. Their pretenses as an English royal and the lost heir to the French throne would fool no one in urban centers. Yet their audiences in small river towns seem so desperate for amusement that they pay to see the men perform and are always wildly disappointed when the men act (badly) for a small amount of time, then sneak off with the ticket money. The real-life Dauphin (son of King Louis XVI of France) supposedly escaped, so many imposters did turn up. As for the "Duke of Bridgewater," his made-up linage is just ridiculous. Once Huck and Jim are hooked up with them, they are taken in by their lifestyle, for what seems an endless time.

Aunt Sally and Uncle Silas Phelps

Aunt Sally is the sister of Aunt Polly, the woman who raises Tom Sawyer in St. Petersburg. Both are sisters of Tom's late mother. Sally has not seen Tom in so many years that when Huck happens onto her place, she assumes he is Tom, arrived for an overdue visit! Sally and Silas are also slave owners, but otherwise compassionate people. Aunt Polly and the real Tom show up to solve the mystery of identity.

Tom Sawyer

Critics wonder why Tom Sawyer had to take the spotlight in the final act of what is Huckleberry Finn's book. Tom becomes tedious and annoying with his endless silly plan, based on romance novels like *The Prisoner of Zenda*, to free the imprisoned Jim. But after fully examining the plot, we will see what Mark Twain was trying to do by including Tom's character.

The Story of Huckleberry Finn Rambles Like the River

Many classic stories take the hero on a journey or a quest. Stumbling blocks arise to the journey, threats are made, even near disasters must be overcome. Huckleberry Finn's story is both Huck's quest to "steal" Jim out of slavery (and save himself from his evil father) and a journey that helps him develop the courage and moral judgment of a young adult.

The story's action begins with a look at Huck's life as we left him at the end of *Tom Sawyer*. He is adopted, civilized, and sent to school. The money Huck and Tom recovered from a deceased robber's hideout is invested so the boys can live a secure life.

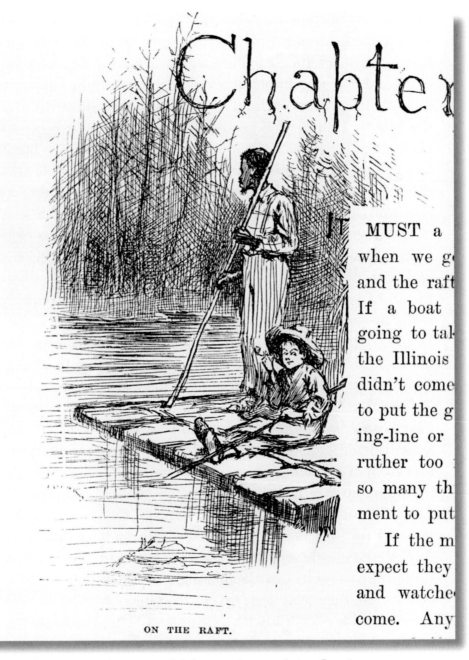

IT MUST a
when we g
and the raft
If a boat
going to tal
the Illinois
didn't come
to put the g
ing-line or
ruther too
so many th
ment to put

If the m
expect they
and watche
come. Any

ON THE RAFT.

An illustration shows Huckleberry Finn and Jim floating on a
raft—Huck smokes and fishes while Jim does the work.

The first section starts by showing Huck adjusting to the Widow Douglas and Miss Watson's ways, until the arrival of his long-absent father, Pap Finn, upsets everyone. Pap harasses Huck and tries to get hold of his money, to which he has some legal claim as Huck's parent. A foolish judge refuses to give the Widow Douglas full custody of Huck. Huck becomes so frightened of Pap, who "said he'd cowhide me till I was black and blue, if I didn't raise some money for him,"[12] that he asks the judge to get rid of his fortune. This section ends when Pap snatches Huck, and takes him 3 miles (4.8 km) upriver to a deserted shack on the Illinois shore. For a time, being held captive is tolerable, since Huck can laze around, smoking his pipe, fishing, never accomplishing anything. However, when the drunken Pap beats Huck and locks him up for long periods while he goes away, the boy realizes he must escape before he either starves, freezes, gets shot, or dies of loneliness. He manages to kill a pig, spread its blood on the cabin floor as if he were killed himself, and float away in an abandoned canoe.

The next section of the plot involves Jim, Miss Watson's slave. Huck finds Jim hiding out on an island. Jim has run away, fearing Watson may have to sell him South, keeping him from ever rescuing his wife and children. After camping on the island together, they decide they should head down to Cairo, Illinois, then use the Ohio River as the road into free territory for Jim. As they prepare the canoe, a huge rainstorm causes a raft to float by their island. They make it their new means of transport. Days later, a night of fog throws them off course, and they miss their exit to the Ohio River. They keep sailing until they collide with a steamboat. After Huck and Jim are forced to swim to shore, they become separated.

In the following section, Huck lands in the middle of a two-family feud. The Grangerford family takes him in while continuing their fight with their neighbors, the Shephersons. As he takes shelter with these people, Huck demonstrates his growing skill at lying about his situation. His faked name and background help him feel secure that his father will not be able to track him down. He starts to feel torn about stealing Jim into freedom because Jim is, after all, still Miss Watson's "property." But he knows he is Jim's only hope in the world. When they are reunited, Huck tells us, "Jim grabbed me and hugged me he was so glad to see me....he says 'Lawsy I's mighty glad to git you back again, honey.'"[13] Together they shove off, trying to avoid any slave catchers until they get back to the Ohio. The next part keeps the reader stuck, along with Huck and Jim, in the fraudulent business of the "entertainers" known as the Duke and the Dauphin. Huck and Jim rescue the two creeps as they are pursued by angry townsmen gunning for them. Huck becomes involved with the Wilks family and a death which leaves a large inheritance to relatives in England. This section becomes complicated and full of deceptions. However, Huck does not abandon the con men, and even thinks of himself as a coworker. The adventure of being a real crook as opposed to one of Tom Sawyer's make-believe robbers sucks him in.

When they hit a river town in Arkansas, Huck says, "We struck it mighty lucky. There was going to be a circus there that afternoon, and the country people were beginning to come in...so our show would have a pretty good chance. The duke hired the court house, and we went around and stuck up our bills [advertisements]."[14] Huck is now fully involved with the con.

At last Huck gets together with Jim, who lays low to avoid being sold as a runaway. He begs Huck to dump the Duke and the Dauphin, saying "I doan hanker for no mo' un um, Huck. Dese is all I kin stand." Jim's instincts are right. When Huck hears Jim moan for his family, he observes, "I do believe he cared just as much for his people as white people do for theirn. It don't seem natural, but I reckon its so."[15] Yet Huck still does not escape the con men.

The pair in the guise of the heirs from England start selling the Wilks property and their slaves to "nigger traders." Of course, the true heirs, Harvey and William Wilks, turn up and stop the fraud just in time. Once Huck sees justice done for the Wilks family, he and Jim escape on the raft. Almost. As the Duke and the Dauphin jump aboard, Huck is stuck with them again.

The pair trick Jim and try to sell him behind Huck's back to the Phelps family, who are relatives of Tom Sawyer. Now Huck fully faces the situation. He has foolishly risked Jim's life, and owes it to Jim to steal him back into freedom.

In the final part of the story Huck is mistaken by the Phelpses for Tom Sawyer. When the real Tom shows up, he eagerly joins this scam, pretending to be his half brother Sid. Tom's grand scheme to free Jim, who is hardly secured at all, becomes an episode in Great Escapes in Literature. Huck goes along with it, although reluctantly, and Jim is stuck in the middle. Tom's real Aunt Polly finally arrives and stops the charade, forcing Tom to admit that Jim has been freed in the will of his owner Miss Watson, who recently passed away.

The ending of Huck's memoir, called "Chapter the Last," provides a dramatic explanation by Tom as to what he had planned to do with the now-free Jim. Of course Tom had one more wild idea: the boys would "run him down the river, on the raft, have adventures plumb to the mouth of the river, then tell him about his being free, and take him back up home on a steamboat in style, and pay him for his lost time."[16] He envisioned all the black people of St. Petersburg on the landing, with a torchlight procession and a brass band, saluting Jim as the hero he truly was.[17] As usual, Tom makes himself the center of the plan, and never asks Jim, a free man for the first time, how he will achieve his goal of reuniting his family. Then Jim relieves Huck of his final fear, a reappearance of Pap Finn, by revealing his own secret. Back up river during a flood, Jim looked into a floating cabin and found Finn's dead body. The great river has washed away one of fiction's darkest characters.

Huck is now truly as free as Jim. Huck—a boy turning into a man—says his final thought is to "light out to the Territory," meaning he will explore the West, seeking his own destiny.

Themes: Universal Ideas in *Huckleberry Finn*

Racism and Slavery: Was Jim Property or a Man?

The story of Jim the runaway slave was already a common one by the Civil War. True narratives by enslaved Americans like Olaudah Equiano (1798), Frederick Douglass (1845), and Solomon Northrup (1853) were joined by the fictional slave, Uncle Tom, created by Harriet Beecher Stowe in 1856. These best-selling books fired the abolition movement. Of course they were not read by slaveholders. To their way of thinking, these books were horrible propaganda. After the Emancipation Proclamation and the end of the Civil War, would America be interested in another tale of an escaping slave?

Scholar Shelley Fisher Fishkin notes that Mark Twain held slave narratives in his personal library and referred to them in his letters and conversations.[18] Twain always remembered the actions of his boyhood friend Ben Blankenship, a wild, undisciplined youth who hid a runaway slave on a river island, and was certainly influenced by this boy's courage when he wrote the tale of Huck and Jim. As biographer Albert Paine says

THE ORIGINS OF TERMS FOR BLACK AMERICANS

The use of derogatory terms for African Americans in Twain's work has long been a source of controversy. Consider this brief history by David Pilgrim: he notes that the Latin word *niger,* which means black, was used for Africans in early centuries. The noun "Negro" came to mean a black person in English. In Spanish and Portuguese *negro* was the word for the color black. In French *negre* and *negress* meant black man and woman. "Nigger" became slang mispronunciation of "Negro" through the nineteenth century. It was commonly used for black people, until it became a "loaded" or negative term. Over the years, the use of the term has caused the book to be banned from schools and libraries across the country.

about Blankenship, "Hiding his runaway negro in an Illinois swamp, [he] could not dream that his humanity would one day supply the moral episode in an immortal book."[19]

What slaves endured to be free was a theme Twain always believed should be discussed and remembered, given the huge amount of racial prejudice still rampant in the nation.

Moral Education: Was Huck Taught Twisted Christianity?

During the first half of *Huckleberry Finn,* Huck sees white men engage in a lot of illegal, even evil behavior. No family members have taught him wrong from right. Huck's mother is dead, and Pap Finn has not a true Christian bone in his body. Huck has had to lie and almost make himself up, day by day, to survive. The Duke and the Dauphin are con men, frauds that leech off everyone, even a young boy like Huck. The only Christians Huck knows—Widow Douglas, Aunt Polly, and

Miss Watson—teach him that to steal a person's property is such a great sin that he will go to hell if he does it.

This confused Christianity puts Huck in a dilemma—one that Mark Twain faced regarding his own family slaves. First Huck considers what would be the best action for the runaway Jim. If he turns him in to his owner Miss Watson, she might be so angry that she sells him "down the river." On the other hand, "If she didn't everybody naturally despises an ungrateful nigger, and they'd make Jim feel it all the time, so he'd feel ornery and disgraced."[20] Huck is also concerned that by aiding Jim, "It would get all around that Huck Finn helped a nigger to get to freedom," which would be a great shame to Huck. He admits he was "stealing a poor old woman's nigger, that ain't never done me no harm."[21] Would Huck send himself to the everlasting fire for this sin?

This "Christian" value system of Huck's childhood should leave him only one course: he must turn Jim in. Yet he can't do it. He weighs the goodness of Jim in always trying to help him and care for him, and faces the truth: he is Jim's only friend. If the other Christians are right, Huck will likely go to hell for stealing Jim out of slavery, but he will risk it. He rids himself of the con men at last, "I'd seen all I wanted to of them, and wanted to get entirely shut of them,"[22] and throws his lot in with Jim.

Huck is told near the very end of the story that Jim has protected him from the painful experience of seeing the decrepit corpse of his own father. Jim must have known that to carry that image of his father for the rest of his life would be a burden for the boy—one more that Jim puts on his own back. Huck, who has never gotten any physical or emotional protection, accepts this protection from Jim without comment.

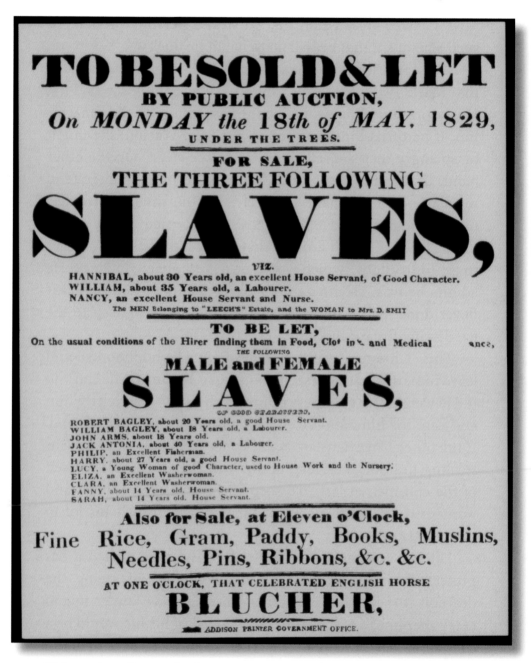

This notice of an early slave auction announces slaves can be both bought and hired out.

Folk Traditions, Superstitions, and Talismans: Did They Protect the Poor and Enslaved?

Huck—and Mark Twain—show great interest in superstitions, both those practiced by white and black people. Jim is a master at using folk tradition and superstition to create a system of rules and protections. A slave had little actual protection under white law—although in some states it was illegal to actually murder one. So men like Jim created their own illusion that if they carefully observed the signs and behaviors of folk superstitions, they could navigate the present and see the future. This gave the poor and enslaved a belief system to carry on with their lives.

Jim has faced a hard truth in the beginning of Huck's story: he must escape before Miss Watson may be forced to sell him downriver, where he will never reunite with his family. No amount of talismans, chanting, and folk behaviors can save him from that fate. Only his personal courage—and his faith in the social outcast Huckleberry Finn—can move him forward.

Retreating into Games and Fantasies: A Theme of *Tom Sawyer* that Ends in *Huck Finn*

Bringing Tom Sawyer back to complicate the ending of Huck's story—and Aunt Polly to stop the nonsense and end the book—has bothered many critics. Biographer Ron Powers thinks Tom's farcical attempts to "free" Jim might represent "the torments visited on former slaves during the post-Reconsruction era."[23] Mark Twain didn't state his reasons, but he carefully considered endings to his books. It seems likely Twain had two reasons for this ending.

First, Mark Twain wanted the novels *Tom Sawyer* and *Huckleberry Finn* to always be linked in peoples' minds, and in sales. It is likely that by the end of the nineteenth century, most American homes had copies of both books side by side. Twain also made notes about a third book that covered Huck and Tom's adventures as teenage boys exploring the Wild West, although he never wrote it.

A second reason may be that Mark Twain wanted us to remember how different Huck and Tom really were in terms of their characters, their conscience, and their courage. Tom is still a boy, full of mischief, fantasies, and games. He represents the average white boy of the 1840s who looked at a slave as a treasured family horse or dog—a useful creature he is fond of, but does not in any way consider an equal human being. Huck is maturing in this book, beyond most white boys of his time. He does not have to belong to Tom's fantasy "robber gang" because he has consorted with real robbers, the Duke and the Dauphin. He no longer treats Jim as a family pet, but as a man struggling to control his life and buy back his family. Huck has at several points in the book actually helped and saved people. If Tom had not played out his endless Great Escape plot, we would have no way to compare how far Huck has advanced beyond his overimaginative younger pal.

The Symbol of the Mississippi River: It Just Keeps Rolling Along

Great novels involving journeys of the hero often contain some kind of natural symbol. Some have mountains to climb, or deserts to cross, or jungles to endure, or seas to navigate. Tom Sawyer and Huckleberry Finn have the mighty Mississippi River. The river does not care that on its east bank people are free and on its west bank people are enslaved. It does not notice if the vessels that ride on its back are humble canoes, patched-together rafts, flat freight barges, or mighty paddle-wheeling steamships. The river gives people a chance to take

SHOWBOAT THE NOVEL, AND THE MUSICAL WITH ONE IMMORTAL SONG

American author Edna Ferber set her novel *Showboat* on a floating paddle wheeler that acted as theater and home for its players and gamblers. Published in 1926 but set in the 1880s, this book reminded Americans of what Mark Twain had written about life on the Mississippi. A Broadway musical version came out in 1927, with music by Jerome Kern and lyrics and book by Oscar Hammerstein II. Both men were Easterners, not familiar with the river culture or the black people who worked the barges. Yet they wrote one perfect song, sung by an 1880 black laborer in his own dialect. It is called "Ol' Man River," a magnificent tribute to the meaning and symbol of the Mississippi and the flow of life itself.

> Ol' man river, Dat ol' man river
>
> He must know sumpin', But he don't say nothin,'
>
> He jes keeps rollin', he keeps on rollin along.
>
> He don't plant taters, he don't plant cotton,
>
> And them that plants 'em is soon forgotten.
>
> But ol' man river, he jes keeps rollin' along.

Later in the song, the laborer says:

> Ah gits weary and sick of tryin'—
>
> Ah'm tired of living and skeered of dyin'—
>
> But ol' man river, he jes keeps rollin' along.
>
> Don't look up, and don't look down.
>
> You dast not make the white boss frown.
>
> Bend your knees and bow your head, An pull dat rope until your dead.

He then sings about another river, the River Jordan, which he longs to cross into eternal freedom. But until then, the Mississippi is all he has. So he repeats:

> Ol man river, Dat ol' man river,
>
> He must know sumpin, but don't say nuthin,
>
> He jes keeps rollin', he keeps on rollin' along.[24]

their journey, although dangers, deep channels, and swift currents are always threatening them. If you have the skill and courage, the river will take you from the very top of America to its southernmost port. And if you were a slave like Jim, the river could be your ticket to freedom.

Critics Argue over *Huckleberry Finn* for 130 Years

So much criticism has been leveled at *Huckleberry Finn* that entire books have been written on these arguments. In many cases, critics criticized other critics! In the late nineteenth century, some critics liked the book, while others complained that the narrative voices of Huckleberry and Jim were too plain and low-class, not even using correct grammar. This must mean, they argued, that the book was not true literature. In the twentieth century, critics became upset that Huckleberry and the rest of his crowd in the 1840s used the word "nigger" to mean black slave. We know now that Twain had his reasons for making the book as authentic as possible—including using slang and racial terms that were common then, but are now out of favor. Critics were also put off by the amount of violence and the criminal elements in the book, although Twain could have assured them that life on the river in the 1840s was exactly as he portrayed it.

Hopefully we who live in the twenty-first century can appreciate that out of all of Twain's books, *Huckleberry Finn* gives us the truest picture of a boy growing up mentally and morally during a difficult time. Many authors in Twain's own century came to revere the book, including the famous novelist Robert Louis Stevenson. He wrote, "It is a book I have read four times and am quite ready to begin again tomorrow."[25]

A Passion for Technology Leads Twain to *A Connecticut Yankee in King Arthur's Court*

During the late 1880s, after he published *Adventures of Huckleberry Finn*, Mark Twain became interested in new machines and technology. He celebrated his fiftieth birthday in 1885, a year in which, as biographer Forrest Robinson says, "his health was good, his family was happy…and he was rolling in money."[1] Along with the popular *Huck Finn*, Twain also published an autobiography of Ulysses S. Grant, the major general who secured the Union Army victory in the Civil War, and the eighteenth president of the United States. Titled *The Personal Memoirs of Ulysses S. Grant*, this amazing autobiography was considered one of America's best pieces of military literature. The memoirs contributed greatly to the security of Grant's family as well as Mark Twain's wife and children. Twain's lecture tours were profitable as well. Friends said Twain remained slim, his red hair still glowing, his blue-green eyes gleaming under his branching eyebrows, and his wit as sharp as ever.

It seemed as if nothing could derail Twain from the road to success. Nothing, that is, except his passion for investing in

Mark Twain, circa 1880

machinery. Around 1880, he began investing with a machinist named James Paige, who was working on a breakthrough in typesetting for printing books. Paige had his machine shop in the Samuel Colt firearms factory in Hartford, Connecticut. The Paige Typesetter never seemed to work as it was promised. However, Twain, who had always been fascinated with the printing process, kept believing. Over a decade later he had dumped much of his family fortune into James Paige and his never-quite-right machine.

Along with continually losing his money, Twain was losing the strength in his right hand and arm to arthritis. He had handwritten the first draft of all his books and stories. He tried dictation with a recording machine, but hated it. He said he had to write by hand, although he was able to do some stretches with his left to relieve his right.

Although writing smaller works would have been easier on him, Twain had already dreamed up a new novel. He had found a copy of Thomas Malory's *Le Morte d'Arthur*, a romance about an ancient King called Arthur, his queen, and his knights. As he read it, Twain envisioned an interesting contrast between the lives of the people in King Arthur's day with a time traveler from nineteenth-century America. His early notes explored how different warfare would be: "Have a battle between [Arthur's knights and] a modern army with gattling guns...600 shots a minute, torpedoes, balloons, 100-ton cannon, ironclad fleet."[2]

In 1887, Twain reopened his notes on the King Arthur novel and began to shape them into something more than a dark satire on British feudalism, like *The Prince and the Pauper*. It would have more adult attitudes and harsher criticism. But what would be the purpose of this new book? Not just a rant on the unfairness of the gap between royals and peasants. It would be a complicated look at the supposed society of King Arthur's day, but with plenty of references to Twain's own society and its absurdities and injustices on the part of the time traveler. He noted that slavery was prevalent in the British isles, as was a dependence on superstition and the supernatural. Twain knew this was not so far from nineteenth-century America. Spiritualism—a belief in the ability to make contact with the spirits of the dead—was immensely popular. And although the United States had abolished slavery, something almost as terrible had taken its place. Prejudice against black people led to a practice called lynching, which meant hanging someone without a trial or sentence. During 1889, the year *A Connecticut Yankee in King Arthur's Court* was finished, "ninety-four African Americans are known to have been lynched."[3] Twain hoped that both the sharp contrasts and similarities in his work would in some ways generate humor as well as make people think.

In 1888, while writing *A Connecticut Yankee*, Twain visited Thomas Edison in his New Jersey laboratory.[4] What he learned about the present and future uses of electricity from the master inventor would come in handy when plotting this book. In the same year, Twain received an honorary master of arts degree from Yale University. For a man who at age twelve made a deal with his mother to take any paying jobs available rather than spend one more day in a school, this must have been an overwhelming experience. It showed how seriously Twain's work was taken.

A Connecticut Yankee Glorifies the Mechanical Age

When Mark Twain began to draft *A Connecticut Yankee in King Arthur's Court*, he thought the workingman was "the rightful sovereign of this world."[5] He believed in the future of the machine culture. It would help people stuck in the under-class achieve equality. His new hero in this book would be not only an imaginative mechanic, but also a labor organizer. He would reform King Arthur in his vision of progress.

Memorable Characters Join the Arthurian Legend

Hank Morgan

Hank is the narrator/storyteller of this novel. A young factory superintendent from Hartford, Connecticut, in the 1870s. He is knocked unconscious and takes a time trip back thirteen centuries into King Arthur's Britain. Although Hank has no idea where he has landed—perhaps an insane asylum?—he soon gets over the fact that it is the year 598, and he may never see his friends in Connecticut again. Smart and determined, Hank believes he can reform this crude medieval society in which he has been placed.

Clarence

A boy who grows into a clever assistant to Hank, Clarence shows how quickly the young can learn new and better ways to live. He begins as a nervous slave to Sir Kay, and ends as a man able to rule the world with equality.

Sir Kay

A knight and lord, also foster brother to King Arthur. First to capture—and exploit—Hank Morgan, Sir Kay is an example of knighthood gone wrong.

Merlin the Magician

A ruthless practicer of black arts who plays on King Arthur's belief in magic spells to protect him. Merlin feels threatened by Hank, who uses "modern" science to work his miracles.

LE MORTE D'ARTHUR: TRUTH OR HISTORIC FICTION?

Thomas Malory used the myths and legends of Wales to create his book *Le Morte d'Arthur*, or *The Death of Arthur*. He wrote it from 1469–1470, and the first edition by an English printer named Caxton came out in 1485. Scholars think it is the first major work of prose written in English. Another more accurate version than Caxton's was discovered in 1934, and edited by Eugene Vinaver. Thomas Malory lived in the mid-fifteenth century, when rulers of Britain rose and fell as did King Arthur in Camelot. During Malory's day, Henry VI was king. But in 1471, Henry VI was murdered, and Edward IV was restored to the throne.

King Arthur was supposed to have ruled during 400–500 CE. Yet no scholars have ever proved he existed at that time or later. Welsh historians blended the stories of several warrior-kings and their famous battles to create Arthur and his Round Table of knights. French author Chrétien de Troyes expanded the tales of Arthur's knights, and added the search for the mysterious Holy Grail to the story in the second half of the twelfth century. Malory's long fifteenth-century version is considered the most complete. *Le Morte d'Arthur* assured that the power of the myth of King Arthur would never die.

When King Arthur tries to banish him, Hank keeps Merlin "in business."

Alisande (Sandy)

A young lady out of the tales in which knights slay dragons and rescue kidnapped princesses, Sandy enlists Hank to go on a quest with her and ends up winning his heart.

**King Arthur, Queen Guinevere, Sir Lancelot,
Sir Gawain, Sir Galahad, Sir Sagramore,
King Urien, Prince Uwaine, and Morgan le Fay**

All of these noble characters are taken straight from Malory's *Morte d'Arthur*. Twain gives each of them his own spin with descriptions like this one for the sorceress Morgan le Fay (who unfortunately shares Hank Morgan's name): "All her ways were wicked, all her instincts devilish. She was loaded to the eyelids with cold malice...I was curious to see her, as curious as I could have been to see Satan."[6] King Arthur, however, is portrayed as basically honest. Willing to learn and broaden his horizon, he takes a humiliating trip through his kingdom to understand his true role as monarch.

Main Action Points Follow a Long and Winding Road

Possibly the best way to follow this complicated book is by thinking of it in sections.

Section One: Hank Arrives and Survives

Hank establishes himself as a newcomer to Camelot with great magical powers. As he is about to be hung for his strange appearance and defiance of Sir Kay, Hank remembers that a solar eclipse is about to occur. He impresses King Arthur by claiming that his magic is about to blot out the sun, and then make it reappear. He succeeds in being named the principal minister to King Arthur, which angers Merlin the magician. His goal becomes to educate Camelot.

Section Two: Hank Sets Up the Factory

After he figures out that the sixth century is completely ignorant of modern weapons or machinery, Hank gets a "factory" going in which he can manufacture everything from gunpowder to explosives. His greatest invention, even though the common man can't read, is the public newspaper. He reasons that now that they have something to read, they will learn! He discovers the main entertainment in King Arthur's court, called jousting with a lance, is a kind of dueling in which the losing knight often dies. After trying to master life in armor—a hilarious misery—Hank changes everything by inventing the gun. He also teaches a team of young men how to turn out water pumps, tools, and other implements to improve the quality of life for the average villager. He even runs a school to teach modern English.

Frontispiece, 1889 edition of *A Connecticut Yankee in King Arthur's Court*

Section Three: Hank and Sandy Go on a Quest

Hank and Sandy ride out to save some supposed princesses who have been captured by ogres and turned to swine. Hank knows it is nonsense but is already fond of Sandy, so they "save' the princess-pigs. While on this quest, Hank also restores a necessary water source which supposedly was destroyed by demons, curses, and other superstitions. He sends for a water pump from his factory and keeps his reputation as master magician when it works.

Section Four: Hank Brings King Arthur on a Search for Knowledge

Hank persuades Arthur to disguise himself as a common peasant to see how his people must live. Arthur agrees, only to find he has lost all power, and ends up being sold into slavery along with Hank. The action becomes complicated with slave drivers, other slaves, attempted escapes, and planned executions of the slaves (including the king!). Hank and Arthur are rescued by Sir Lancelot and his knights who make enough speed by riding something Hank invented for long rides: bicycles! Arthur returns to his throne and sets out to abolish slavery.

Section Five: Hank Fights Sir Sagramore to Remain in Power

This section shows the power of the simplest weapon, a cowboy's lasso, as compared to the most complex, revolvers and cannons. His weapons are all it takes for Hank to challenge the knights in England. Sadly, when he tries to explain the concept of modern law and government, it impresses the people, but angers the one institution he can't reform: the Catholic Church.

Section Six: To Get Rid of Hank, the Church Publishes "The Interdict" to Cause Revolution

Three years later, Hank and Sandy are married with a daughter. In an awkward plot turn, when Hank's baby falls ill with a disease, doctors tell him to take his family to France where the baby will have a better chance for recovery. Hank and Sandy believe them and go, but this leaves England without Hank's powerful leadership. This is actually a ploy by the Catholic Church. While Hank is absent, Sir Lancelot and Queen Guinevere's relationship is revealed, which so angers King Arthur that he wages war on Lancelot and his force of knights. The church publishes something called "The Interdict," which causes most people to revolt against Hank.

Section Seven: Hank's War to Save Camelot

The finale of the book is quite chaotic. Hank returns and Clarence builds an army out of fifty-two young men trained to use all of Hank's weapons. They use Merlin's Cave as their storage area. When the church sends an army of knights against them, Hank, Clarence, and the cadets win with superior fire power. The irony is that they are trapped by a wall of dead bodies, and when disease sets in, Hank and most of his men die. We never find out the fate of the common people that Hank tried to elevate and save.

Supposedly Hank and Clarence have left a written testimony of his time in Camelot, which is found thirteen hundred years later with the "real" Hank on his deathbed, dreaming of Sandy. He believes he may have returned to Camelot, thinks he hears King Arthur coming...and dies.

The Tone of the Book Shifts:
Hilarious Excess vs. Serious Social Criticism

As we can see by looking through the plot points, *A Connecticut Yankee* is a book that uses wildly different styles and tones. An example of how Twain contrasts the crude manners and inhumane disregard for human life with the often amusing behavior of folks in 598 CE can be seen in chapter seventeen, "A Royal Banquet." While on their quest, Hank, Sandy, and Clarence are entertained in King Urien's court. Hank counts the royals, officers, and family members as "altogether about a hundred and eighteen persons sitting, and about as many liveried [uniformed] servants standing behind their chairs or serving...it was a very fine show!" The band's songs, however, are unimpressive. "For some reason the queen had the composer hanged, after dinner."[7] The "mighty feeding" was massive, and the huge roasted wild boar was eaten so completely that "nothing was left but the semblance of a hoop skirt."[8] Then the heavy drinking begins, and the telling of rude jokes that delight men and women alike. By midnight "everyone was sore with laughing...drunk, some weeping, some affectionately, some hilariously, some quarrel-somely, some dead under the table."[9]

The evening ends for Hank when Queen Morgan le Fay offers him one of her favorite amusements: he can watch a man "torn asunder" on the rack. At this point the tone moves back from exaggerated fooling to cruel treatment. The man on the rack's crime? "He had been accused by an anonymous informer of having killed a stag on the royal preserves."[10] Morgan is forced to see the prisoner tortured, his young wife and baby huddled in the corner. The prisoner tells Morgan the truth. He did kill the deer to feed his hungry family.

103

The law dictates that he may be tortured to death, but if he never confesses, his home can not be taken away, and his wife and child turned to beggars. At this dark moment, Morgan starts to use his famous powers as a "magician" for good. He demands the couple be turned over to him, where they will go to his colony—a "Factory where I'm going to turn groping and grubbing automata into men."[11]

In one evening, Twain has shifted the tone of the book from satirical observations, bawdy jokes, and drunken fool-ishness to the dark cruelty of the law against the poor. Few authors did this kind of shifting so successfully. Most novels were dramas or comedies, romances or fantasies. Only Twain could change his tone so continually, for which there was no descriptive genre. Because of its time-traveling, and the way the action concludes in a consummation that sounds like the end of the world, this may make the book "the first American science-fiction novel."[12]

Not until the 1950s did novelists take up this wild shifting of tone in their writing. Norman Mailer, Joseph Heller, and Kurt Vonnegut are three American authors who may have been influenced by Mark Twain in their style.

Five Main Themes

A Connecticut Yankee examines many areas of human development and behavior. As we read through the novel, we see Twain developing five important themes to explore.

Equal Rights of Man Compared to Divine Right of Kings

The concept of equal rights was unheard of in western civilization at the time in which the story is set. Until the nineteenth century, when America became a republic and was followed by several European governments, everyone accepted rule by

King Arthur, seated on his throne, observes Merlin and the Knights
of the Round Table.

a line of monarchs. Even when parliaments were formed, the monarch had great power. Hank Morgan believes in the equal rights of all classes, although the peasants have miles to go before they can be rid of fear and superstition and make use of their rights. He states in chapter twenty-five that it is a self-proved fact that "even the best-governed and most free and most enlightened monarchy is still behind the best condition attainable by its people."[13]

Laws of Modern Science Compared to Dogmas of Organized Religion

In the sixth century little scientific knowledge existed in print, even for those who could read. Almost all knowledge was recorded in books by the Catholic Church, and it was kept there. Mark Twain suspected that the church had hidden scientific research if it threatened church dogma. Hank Morgan decides in chapter sixteen that even introducing the use of soap would threaten the church, being a step forward. "Next, education, next, freedom, and then she would begin to crumble...any Established Church is an established crime, an established slave pen."[14] But not to worry about Twain being too angry and serious here—he jumps right into his soap crusade, where his "missionaries" get the nobles not to fear using soap by giving it a test bath on their dog.[15] At the end of chapter thirty-five, however, Hank admits that the church may have at least one holy priest. A mother who was about to be hung cried out that her baby would die. "It has no home, it has no father, no friend, no mother." A good priest tells her, "It has them all! All these I will be to it till I die."[16] Hank comments, "The mother carried her gratitude away to the treasury of heaven, where all things that are divine belong."[17]

Freedom Under the Law and Humane Punishments for All

Slavery is a way of life in sixth century Britain, with any sort of captive likely to be enslaved and resold. When King Arthur and Hank Morgan are captured by slavers, they are dressed as peasants and have no way to prove they are free men. Being in a stagnant little town, Hank is sold for nine dollars, and the king of England bought for only seven. Hank ends chapter thirty-four by musing, "It only shows that there is nothing diviner about a king than there is about a tramp, after all...I reckon we are all fools. Born so, no doubt."[18] The concept of humane and righteous punishment is not known to this age either, as we see in many horrible scenes played in dungeons, torture chambers, and poverty-stricken villages. If all in Britain were made free, Hank says, they would eliminate brutal laws. However, "Arthur's people were poor material for a republic, because they had been debased so long by monarchy."[19]

Reality and Illusion: Do We Need Them Both to Live?

Belief in magical spells, superstitions, and spiritualism goes back to tribal societies and is thriving in sixth-century Britain. Hank believes in reality: hard science and good quality machinery. Most of his workers, and his beloved Sandy, respect Hank and address him as "Sir Boss." But they still believe in magic that can turn princesses into pigs, and allow visits from spirits in dreams. After the war concludes, Clarence tells Hank something a knight had told King Arthur: "Remember ye of your night's dream and what the spirit of Sir Gawaine told you this night, yet God of his great goodness hath preserved you thithero. For God's sake, my Lord, leave off by this."[20] Putting Arthur's dream warning, and the power of God's goodness, in the same sentence shows the blending of illusion with true faith that was strong at this time.

The "Past" Sixth Century Compared to the "Present" Nineteenth Century

Has progress has been made and life improved over 1,300 years? Or have we just created better warfare? Hank Morgan cannot make a clear decision by the end of what modern critics remind us is "a singularly adult novel."[21] He is proud that the new Camelot has steamships and warships, and the start of a steam commercial marine. He even has plans to discover America. In three years Camelot is on its way to becoming Connecticut. Yet the weaknesses that always reside in the human heart and spirit live on, and these improvements don't guarantee a great enduring society.

Is Hank Morgan a Representative of Modern Man—or Mark Twain Himself?

Readers realize after reading *A Connecticut Yankee* that Hank Morgan is a complex, changeable man who develops through the course of the story. Critic Cari Keebaugh looks at Hank's relationship with Malory's classic characters King Arthur, Sir Lancelot, Merlin, and others, and says, "Unique interactions with legendary fictional heroes make Hank a deep, complex character, while allowing the reader to more easily access his ambiguities...Twain crafted a hero with contradictory behaviors and beliefs: in short, he created a character who was honestly human."[22] We enjoy Hank's sense of humor and determination to show King Arthur how much better his subjects' lives could be with the benefits of modern knowledge. But we also notice Hank has flaws, and often does not admit to them. Keebaugh states that "Hank's ignorance is exactly what makes him such a timeless character."[23] Perhaps it is also what makes Hank a reflection of Mark Twain? For those who knew him well, Hank reminded them of the author himself. Here are a few of those similarities.

Belief in communication through daily public newspapers. Twain's life-long love was setting, printing, and then writing for the newspapers. The newspaper is one of the first things Sir Boss gets going in Camelot. Of course, he has to get the population reading, which meant:

Public Education for all. Twain hated his small-town school and was stifled by the way he was taught. Yet as he matured and raised his three children in Hartford, he praised the improvements in educating all citizens, no matter what their economic class. Hank Morgan did, too. As soon as some of the population got reading and math skills, Hank moved them into:

Ingenious inventing. Twain was infatuated with inventions, and tried his hand at patenting several products including a self-pasting scrapbook. Hank Morgan learned mechanical invention at the Colt Firearms Factory in Hartford, and brought all his enthusiasm for invention to Camelot. Unfortunately, Hank's best skills turned out to be at inventing weapons. Actual use of weapons for combat was something Twain hated, as did Hank, which we see when he tries:

Jousting and dueling. Twain avoided several duels, a common practice in the mid-nineteenth century. Hank does just as poorly jousting with sword and lance, but does well with lassos and other simple means to stop people from killing him. Twain and Hank could use their ability with fancy phrases and language to stun an adversary, which we see when Hank stops the hangman with:

Word power as effective weapon. Hank's plan of having Lancelot and his knights make fast time to save Arthur and him from hanging by riding in on bicycles succeeds. He yells at his captors, "'On your knee, every rascal of you, and salute the king! Who fails shall sup in hell tonight!'—I always use that high style when I'm climaxing an effect."[24] Twain knew that powerful language and word choice could convince people of anything. He is quoted as saying, "The difference between the right word and the almost right word is the difference between lightning and the lightning bug." Twain—and Hank—found the lightning every time.

THE LATER LIFE OF
SAMUEL CLEMENS AND
WRITINGS OF MARK TWAIN

In 1895, Livy, Clara and Sam Clemens went to England to earn money from a lecture tour. Susy stayed home in Hartford. She became ill just before she was to join them. When it became severe, the family could not sail home in time to be with her. Jean Clemens sat beside Susy as she languished with fever.

Olivia Susan Clemens died on August 18, 1896, of meningitis in the family's Hartford home. Penicillin, which can cure this disease, would not be invented for another thirty-two years. Sam received word by wire in Guildford, England, and said much later, "It is one of the mysteries of our nature that a man unprepared can receive a thunder-stroke like that, and live."[1]

Livy Clemens developed heart disease, and in September 1902 she became ill. She was nursed at home in Riverdale, New York. Clara suspended her singing career, and Jean and Clara became Livy's nursing team. Doctors thought physically being with Sam would be too "exciting" for Livy's heart, so he could only slip lots of notes under her bedroom door, making Livy feel isolated and unhappy.

Twain with daughter Clara (*standing*) and wife Olivia

In December 1902, at age twenty-two, Jean contracted pneumonia. The news of her illness was withheld from Livy. Jean recovered but was weakened.

By the summer of 1903, both Jean and Livy had regained some health. They were taken back to Quarry Farm in Elmira, Livy's family home. Sam had sold their beloved Hartford home that year. He could not afford it, and it was hard to live in a place where Susy had died.

When Livy seemed strong enough, they sailed to Italy for the winter of 1904 with Clara and Jean, and maid Katy Leary. During a bad winter in Italy, Livy got worse. She passed away on June 5, 1904, at only fifty-seven years of age. Heartbroken, Sam said, "I am tired and old. I wish I were with Livy."[2] They buried her by her family's graves in Elmira on July 14.

Jean, who was epileptic, had started to have seizures. For the rest of the summer of 1904, Clara and Jean took a summer house in the village of Lee, in the Berkshire Hills of western Massachusetts. A carriage accident badly hurt Jean. Clara had a sort of nervous breakdown. But they both survived. All Sam could do was continue to write and live with his grief over the loss of Susy and Livy.

In the final years of Jean's life, her mind was affected by her severe epilepsy. She had violent spells in 1906. Sam sent her for treatment in Germany in 1908, but there was no cure for Jean. Sam built a home in western Connecticut called Stormfield after one of his last characters. Clara married there in October 1909, and on Christmas Eve, Jean suffered a grand seizure in the bath there and died.

On April 21, 1910, Samuel Clemens, known to so many as Mark Twain, passed away at Stormfield, with his only surviving family member, Clara, holding his hand. He was seventy-four. He had produced about forty books of fiction, several plays, a great number of short stories, a multitude of essays and sketches, and countless letters treasured by their recipients. Almost everything he wrote remains in print. He received medals and honorary university degrees. He knew many American presidents, most closely Ulysses S. Grant, whose memoir he published. Twain's life and work represented the long struggle to overcome prejudice and bring true equality and freedom to all Americans through emancipation, the Civil War, and Reconstruction. Like Abraham Lincoln, he believed in liberty and justice for all. Perhaps this is why Mark Twain was often called the Lincoln of Literature.

Some Later Books of Mark Twain

Because of requests from many fans of *The Adventures of Tom Sawyer*, Twain wrote two more novels: *Tom Sawyer Abroad* (1894), and *Tom Sawyer, Detective* (1896). These books were intended to be enjoyed by teenage and older readers. In *Tom Sawyer Abroad*, Tom, Huck and Jim take a hot air balloon trip, ending up in the Sahara and the Middle East, mixed up in mystery and adventure. In *Tom Sawyer, Detective*, Huck tells the tale of himself and Tom as they become involved with Jake, a diamond thief, and his two angry cohorts that he has cheated. To add to the mystery, the thief has a twin named Jupiter, who works for Tom's Uncle Silas. The plot gets really twisted, with a murder but no body, thieves who have lost their diamonds, and Tom's uncle put on trial. Can Tom and Huck become detectives and bring justice to all?

Twain also wrote more books that were intended mostly for adults: *The American Claimant* (1892); *The Tragedy of Pudd'nhead Wilson* (1894); *Personal Recollections of Joan of Arc* (1896); *Adam's Diary* (1904); *Eve's Diary* (1906); and *Captain Stormfield's Visit to Heaven* (1909). Each is wonderful in its own way but their style and content are more suitable for grownups.

Where Can We See Mark Twain's Work?

Films

Another way to enjoy Mark Twain's work is on film, some of which go all the way back to 1919 when films were silent. Films can't include all the scenes and dialogue that we find in his great novels, but a film can still bring out the excitement and the fun that Twain intended. Here is a list of some popular films made of the books that we have just studied:

A scene from the 1960 film version of *Adventures of Huckleberry Finn*

Adventures of Huckleberry Finn. In 1960, a good film of this book was made by director Michael Curtiz. It starred Eddie Hodges as Huck, great boxer Archie Moore as Jim, and Tony Randall as The King. Three popular comedians—Andy Devine, Judy Canova, and Buster Keaton—also played roles. A TV movie came out in 1978, and a fine production by the Public Broadcasting System's *American Playhouse* was made in 1985. The Disney Studio also did a nice animated version in 1993.

Huckleberry Finn. Using this title, two more films were produced: in 1974 a musical version featuring Harvey Korman and Paul Winfield as Jim; and in 1975, a TV movie starring Ron Howard and Donny Most of *Happy Days* TV fame.

The Adventures of Tom Sawyer. A good version was done back in 1938 starring Tommy Kelly, Walter Brennan, Victor Jory, and May Robson, but it may be hard to find. In 1973, two films came out: one was a musical version starring child stars Jodie Foster and Johnny Whitaker, and the other was a TV movie starring Buddy Ebsen and Jane Wyatt. A merger of two books, called *Tom and Huck*, was made by Disney Studios in 1995, but the result was far from what Twain wrote, and is not recommended.

The Prince and the Pauper. Only two great film versions were made of this book. In 1937 a film version was made featuring Errol Flynn and Claude Rains, but it will be hard to find. A 1978 film version starred Mark Lester as the boys, with Oliver Reed, George C. Scott, and Rex Harrison, and is highly rated. Many ineffective ripoffs of this book also came out, such as *The Prince and the Surfer*. These kinds of films show us one thing: that Twain's books were so well-loved that they could stand being lampooned.

A Connecticut Yankee in King Arthur's Court. This long and complicated novel had no film version that really captured all of Hank Morgan's adventures. There is a popular film from 1949 starring Bing Crosby as Hank with Rhonda Fleming as Sandy which does tell a lot of the story. Three more films made a botch of it: *A Young Connecticut Yankee in King Arthur's Court, A Kid in King Arthur's Court,* and *A Knight in Camelot,* in which Whoopi Goldberg plays a computer techie. A really weird plot switch version is called *Arthur's Quest,* in which five-year-old Arthur is sent to modern Connecticut, then must return ten years later to save Camelot. Even Mark Twain couldn't have followed this one.

Twain's life has also been put on film. *Ken Burns America* is a series on the Public Broadcasting System. Ken Burns produced and directed a two-part, four-hour film titled *Mark Twain* for this series that covers the author's long and productive life.

Stage Productions

Many play versions are available today of Twain's novels.

The most popular book to dramatize is *The Adventures of Tom Sawyer.* Authors Charles George, Wilbur Braun, Michele Vacca, Timothy Mason, and more have written published adaptations. *Tom Sawyer* made it to Broadway in 2001 with a book by Ken Ludwig and a score by Don Schlitz. It closed, but was revived in 2010 and did well. A nonmusical adaptation was produced by Laura Eason in 2010.

A new play is in development, called *Sawyer* by Noah Altshuler. This young man was awarded the Mark Twain House's "Playwright in Residence" in 2015 when he was only seventeen. His play combines elements of all three of the Tom

Sawyer novels. Plans are in place for 2017 productions of *Sawyer* in London and New York.

Adventures of Huckleberry Finn is the next most popular work for stage productions. *Huck Finn* was written by Greg Banks, who blended elements of Tom Sawyer and Huck together. A delightful version called *Big River*, is a Broadway musical telling the tale of Huck and Jim, set to a superior score by Roger Miller.

Many high-quality scripts also exist for *The Prince and the Pauper* and *A Connecticut Yankee*.

Where Can We Feel Like We Are a Part of Mark Twain's Life?

Four areas where Mark Twain lived have been restored and opened to the public. They allow us to walk in Twain's footsteps and better understand how his life influenced his work. If visiting them personally is not possible, fans of Mark Twain can access their websites, which have many photos, explanations, and virtual tours. They are the following:

The Mark Twain Birthplace State Historic Site. Florida, Missouri. Maintained by the Missouri State Park system in the Mark Twain State Park, this site is where Twain was born and lived until his parents moved to Hannibal. The little cabin where baby Sam was born is gone. But as a toddler, he joined seven other residents tucked into a simple two-room cabin which still exists. At the website www.mostateparks.com, a Twain fan can plan a visit or just enjoy the photos, information, and a fine video presentation. Most interesting items to see include an original handwritten manuscript of *The Adventures of Tom Sawyer*, along with other first editions of Twain works. But don't worry if you can't find the old village of Florida. The video on the website reports that it now only exists as a spot for summer residents and campers.

The Mark Twain Boyhood Home & Museum. Hannibal, Missouri. This busy Mississippi River port has been a very popular spot to explore since Twain died, and annually attracts many tourists. The childhood home of Samuel Clemens (used as a model for Tom Sawyer's house), plus period homes used for other Twain characters are open to his fans. Visitors are self-guided, but staff is present to answer questions. The complex has eight buildings plus a famous statue of Tom and Huck at Cardiff Hill. Henry H. Sweets, the executive director, reported in a letter on November 8, 2016, that "we have been emptying out the Grant's Drug store in preparation for a major restoration." This store is one of the many buildings in town from the 1830s–1840s when Twain was a boy. In the museum's newsletter "The Fence Painter," Sweets is pictured cutting the ribbon to open the new interactive exhibits in the Becky Thatcher House in September 2016.[3] The museum contains many trips back in time, including a replica of the wheel room of a steamboat, just like one Twain would have stood in during his days as a pilot.

The Mark Twain House & Museum. Hartford, Connecticut. This is the home that Sam and Livy Clemens had designed exactly to fit their family needs and lifestyle in 1874 and was their home until they sold it in 1903. Much of the 11,500-square-foot (1,068-square-meter) mansion has been restored to reflect their life in 1870s Hartford. Visitors are helped to picture the Clemens family, their loyal servants, and friends, as they used the parlors, library, dining room, kitchen, playroom for the girls, and bedrooms. Twain's favorite area was the third floor, which he used privately as his billiard room, smoking room, and writing space. Cindy Lovell, director of the house and museum, states in a film shown on their website, "We think it was the original man cave."[4]

Livy Clemens wanted the latest 1874 comforts for her family, and this included outfitting the seven bathrooms with indoor plumbing, and hot and cold water. Most houses at this time had none of these conveniences. The twenty-five rooms were lit by gaslight, another innovation. Later, Sam had a burglar alarm security system installed that operated on batteries. We assume it made a great racket if set off, but no wiring existed to notify police. Twain wrote about this development in his home life in a story titled "The McWilliamses and the Burglar Alarm."

The Mark Twain House in Hartford, Connecticut

Lovell explained in an interview that restoration is ongoing at the house museum. On December 4, 2016, the house officially opened the Best Guest Room, or the Mahogany Room. This restored dressing room, bedroom, and bath suite was reserved for household guests. Livy sometimes used it as a gift-wrapping room, and Susy, Clara, and Jean kept props and costumes in its dressing room for their family theatricals. Another ongoing restoration area is the Carriage House barn where the family carriage horses, cows, and other animals were kept. This space also opened on December 4, 2016. New also in 2016, said Lovell, are historic interpreters who do living history tours. Character actors portray people who once lived in the house.

A new museum center adjoins the Mark Twain House & Museum where visitors can enjoy changing historic exhibits such as a 2016 one exploring the true personalities of the three Clemens daughters. This building also has the museum store, an auditorium for regularly held presentations, and classrooms for special programs on literature and writers workshops. The large grounds which border the Harriet Beecher Stowe Center are used for community celebrations. Day to day activities can be noted on the Facebook page titled The Mark Twain House & Museum.

The Center for Mark Twain Studies at Elmira College, and Quarry Farm. Elmira, New York. Olivia Langdon Clemens came from a prosperous family in Elmira. During her marriage, her sister Susan and brother-in-law Theodore Crayne owned Quarry Farm. Olivia married Sam there, and returned to have each of her babies. The Crayne's three children played with the Clemens girls every summer. At this time, the farm buildings are not open to the public. You can take a virtual tour of the grounds and interior by visiting the

Mark Twain Studies page on the college's website. (See Further Reading for more information.)

One special place at Quarry Farm, now removed to the Elmira College campus for preservation, is open to Twain fans. The family built a special study for Twain, which he described as "a snug little octagonal den with a coal-grate, 6 big windows, one little one, and a wide doorway...On hot days I spread the study wide open, and anchor my papers down with brickbats."[5] This structure gave Twain a private work space during the family's visits. And work he did. With almost no distractions he got more consistent writing done in the Quarry Farm study than any other place. He resumed work on *Huckleberry Finn* in the summer of 1883, and wrote to a friend, "I wrote 4000 words today and I touch 3000 and upwards pretty often...I am away along in a big one that I half finished two or three years ago ...and I shall like it, whether anybody else does or not."[6] Another structure is now open as well. Called The Barn at Quarry Farm, it allows guests to enjoy talks and presentations on Twain topics. (See Quarry Farm's Facebook page for more.)

The Center for Mark Twain Studies at Elmira College is available on request to adult scholars, teachers, and students of Twain's work.

The complete works and papers of Mark Twain are kept at the University of California, Berkeley. This extensive site is what Lovell calls, "delightful, easy to navigate, and crammed full of intimate, engaging, and authentic Clemens."[7]

One final site may be of interest. The members of the Langdon family, as well as Samuel, Olivia, and their four children, are all buried at nearby Woodlawn Cemetery of Elmira, which the public is invited to view.

Twain Talks: Collections of His Witty and Profound Sayings

Mark Twain gave a lifetime of lectures and dinner speeches, along with essays and stories that featured his observations on life. He is quoted endlessly from these sources, but sometimes incorrectly. If we want to get his sayings right, the best website is www.twainquotes.com. Created by expert scholar Barbara Schmidt, this site rounds up all the popular Twain quotes and puts them in categories. The categories are then listed by their first letter in an alphabetized directory. All are substantiated. Here is an example of several of Twain's reflections on the subject of truth:

1. If you tell the truth you don't have to remember anything. (*Notebook*, 1894)

2. Truth is the most valuable thing we have. Let us economize it. (*Following the Equator*)

3. I have not professionally dealt in truth. Many when they come to die have spent all the truth that was in them, and enter the next world as paupers. I have saved up enough [truth] to make an astonishment there! (*Notebook*)

When we read these three quotes on the same subject, we can enjoy Twain looking at it from three different points in life. In the first, a young man, having been instructed to tell the truth, realizes that it is a good idea, since he will never have to remember his lies. In the second, a middle-aged man sees that the truth is a precious commodity, and should be saved up in life. In the last, an older man—Twain himself?—makes fun of his tendency to refrain from telling the truth so that when he goes to heaven, he will have a wealth of truth left to take along!

Mark Twain on the cover of *Time* in 2014. The magazine presented a collection of articles discussing Twain's continuing relevance in modern times.

Although Twain made observations about all areas of life over one hundred years ago, we find that as both a wise and clever man, his quotes are certainly worth reading today. And they are studied and loved by all societies around the world, making him one of the most quoted English-speaking authors alongside William Shakespeare.

Twain Fame! Mark Twain's Popularity Today

Mark Twain was one of the first world travelers who wrote professionally about his experiences. Written in 1869, *The Innocents Abroad*, or *The New Pilgrims' Progress*, according to Cindy Lovell, "is still published and popular around the world. It was his best-selling book while he was alive."[8] More important, Twain's books are found in print in every major language. Even in countries where America may not always be popular, somehow Twain's stories still are. Can it be that he, like all great authors, has transcended his time and place—and has become universal?

CHRONOLOGY

The main source for this chronology is the third edition Norton Critical Edition of *Adventures of Huckleberry Finn*, edited by Thomas Cooley, 1999.

1835– Samuel Langhorne Clemens is born on November 30 in Florida, Missouri, to Jane Lampton Clemens and John Marshall Clemens.

1839– Family moves to Hannibal, Missouri; father is a merchant and justice of the peace.

1847-1852– Clemens spends his boyhood in Hannibal; becomes apprenticed to a local printer after death of father; older brother Orion buys Sam's first sketch, "A Gallant Fireman," for his newspaper, the *Western Union*.

1853–1857– Works as printer, and then reporter for newspapers in St. Louis, Philadelphia, Cincinnati, and Keokuk, Iowa.

1857–1861– Is apprenticed to a senior pilot of the riverboat *Paul Jones*; pilots from 1859 to 1861; fights for a few months in a local militia; travels with Orion to Nevada Territory where Orion becomes secretary to the governor.

1862–1864– Tries prospecting and lumbering; returns to newspaper writing in Virginia City, Nevada; begins signing articles "Mark Twain" in February 1863.

1864–1866– Moves to San Francisco; writes for newspaper and sends pieces to other papers across the country; "Jim Smiley and his Jumping Frog" is first published in the New York *Saturday Press*; travels to Hawaii to gain writing and lecture material on "The Sandwich Islands;" sails to New York as correspondent for the San Francisco *Alta California*.

1867–1868— Sails to Europe and the Holy Land; gathers material for his first major book, *The Innocents Abroad.*

1869–1871— *Innocents Abroad* comes out; Twain lives in Buffalo, New York, and writes and lectures; woos and marries Olivia Langdon; they have a son, Langdon, in November.

1871–1877— Rents a home in Hartford, Connecticut; a daughter, Susan Olivia, is born in March 1872; son, Langdon, dies of diphtheria; Twain builds a grand home in Nook Farm; they move in just after Clara Clemens is born in 1874; Twain works on *Huckleberry Finn*; publishes *Roughing It, The Gilded Age, Sketches New and Old*, and *The Adventures of Tom Sawyer.*

1878–1879— Takes Livy, Susy, and Clara on a trip through Europe.

1879–1884— Continues to work on *Huckleberry Finn*; daughter Jean is born in July 1880; publishes *A Tramp Abroad, The Prince and the Pauper*, and *Life on the Mississippi.*

1884— A British edition of *Adventures of Huckleberry Finn* is published in December.

1885— American edition of *Huckleberry Finn* is published.

1886–1900— Publishes *A Connecticut Yankee in King Arthur's Court; The American Claimant; Pudd'nhead Wilson; Tom Sawyer Abroad; Tom Sawyer, Detective; Personal Recollections of Joan of Arc;* and *Following the Equator;* makes a world lecture tour in 1895; daughter Susy dies of meningitis in August 1896 at home in Hartford.

1901— Receives an honorary doctorate of letters from Yale University.

1902— Receives an honorary degree from the University of Missouri. Makes his last trip to see Hannibal.

1903— Sells his Hartford home, takes Livy to Italy for her health.

1904-1908— Livy dies in Italy in June 1904; Twain returns to New York with Jean; receives an honorary degree from Oxford University in England in 1907.

1908-1909— Builds a home in Redding, Connecticut, and calls it Stormfield; daughter Jean dies.

1910— Samuel Clemens—the beloved Mark Twain—dies on April 21 at age sixty-nine. Like all of his family members, he is buried in Elmira, New York.

CHAPTER NOTES

Chapter 1. A Boy Survives on the Western Frontier

1. Ron Powers, *Mark Twain: A Life* (New York: Free Press, 2005), p. 8.
2. Quoting Twain, *The Gilded Age*, reprinted in *The Oxford Mark Twain* (New York: Oxford University Press, 1996), pp. 29–30.
3. Powers, p. 41.
4. Shelley Fisher Fishkin, ed., *A Historical Guide to Mark Twain* (New York: Oxford University Press, 2002), p. 32.
5. Mark Twain, *Mark Twain's Autobiography* (New York: Harper & Bros., 1924), 1:96.
6. Ibid., p. 98
7. Ibid., p. 101.
8. Ibid., pp. 101–102.
9. Ibid., p. 124.
10. Ibid.
11. *Mark Twain's Autobiography*, p. 123.
12. Powers, p. 37.
13. Powers, p. 42.
14. Powers, p. 73.

Chapter 2. Sam's Boyhood Lives Again: *The Adventures of Tom Sawyer*

1. Mark Twain, *The Adventures of Tom Sawyer* (1876; repr., New York, NY: P.F. Collier & Son, 1920), preface.
2. Ibid.
3. Ibid., p. 189.
4. Ibid., p. 90
5. Mark Twain, *Mark Twain's Autobiography* (New York: Harper & Bros., 1924), 1:105.
6. *Tom Sawyer*, p. 287.

7. Ibid., p. 292.

8. William Dean Howells, Review of *Tom Sawyer* in *Atlantic Monthly*, May 1876, University of Virginia Library, 2012, .

9. Moncure Conway, Review of *Tom Sawyer* in *London Examiner*, June 17, 1876, University of Virginia Library, .

10. Review of *Tom Sawyer* in *New York Times*, January 13, 1877, University of Virginia Library, .

Chapter 3. Sam Takes Charge of a Larger Boat

1. Shelley Fisher Fishkin, ed., *A Historical Guide to Mark Twain* (Oxford University Press, 2002), p. 36.

2. Ron Powers, *Mark Twain: A Life* (New York: Free Press, 2005), pp. 94–95.

3. Forrest Robinson, "Mark Twain: A Brief Biography," in *A Historical Guide to Mark Twain*, Shelley Fisher Fishkin, ed. (Oxford: Oxford University Press, 2002), p. 37.

4. Powers, p. 97.

5. Mark Twain, "Mark Twain's Civil War" (Lexington, KY: University of Kentucky Press, 2007).

6. Ibid., p. 47.

7. Ibid., p. 867.

8. Powers, p. 99.

9. Lawrence Howe in Afterword, Mark Twain, *Life on the Mississippi* (New York: Oxford University Press, 1996).

10. Ibid., p. 64.

11. Ibid.

12. Ibid., p. 65.

13. Ibid., p. 70.

14. Ibid.

15. Ibid., p. 77.

16. Ibid., p. 118.

17. Ibid., p. 119.

Chapter 4. Inspiration Comes From the West as Sam Clemens Becomes Mark Twain

1. Ron Powers, *Mark Twain: A Life* (New York: Free Press, 2005), p. 129.
2. Ibid., p. 107.
3. Ibid., p. 108.
4. Shelley Fisher Fishkin, ed., *A Historical Guide to Mark Twain* (New York: Oxford University Press, 2002), p. 37.
5. Ibid.
6. Robinson, *A Historical Guide*, p. 38.
7. "Jim Smiley," Mark Twain, *Collected Tales, Sketches, Speeches & Essays 1852-1890* (New York: Library Classics of the United States, 1992), p. 173.
8. Ibid., p. 175.
9. Mark Twain, *Roughing It* (New York: Oxford University Press, 1996), p. 97.
10. Ibid.
11. Ibid.
12. Ibid., p. 98.
13. Ibid.
14. Ibid.
15. Ibid., p. 109.
16. Ibid., p. 111.
17. Ibid., p. 118.
18. Ibid., Prefatory.
19. Ibid., p. 146.
20. Ibid., p. 149.
21. Powers, p. 318.
22. Ibid., p. 280.
23. Information on the Mark Twain House comes from the house museum's website: www.marktwainhouse.org/The House.

Chapter 5. From Tall Tales to Olde Legends: Twain Moves to the Sixteenth Century

1. Mark Twain, *The Prince and the Pauper. A Tale for Young People of All Ages* (New York: Harper & Brothers Publishers, 1881), preface.
2. Ibid.
3. For further information on the birth and raising of Edward VI, see www.tudorplace.com/ar/aboutEdward.htm.
4. For further information on the rule of Edward VI, see www.bbc.co.uk. Historic Figures.
5. *The Prince and the Pauper*, p. 230.
6. Ibid., p. 234.
7. Ibid., pp. 149–151.
8. Ibid., p. 162.
9. Ibid., p. 165.
10. Ibid., p. 117.
11. Ibid., p. 253.
12. Justin Kaplan, *Mr. Clemens and Mark Twain* (New York: Simon & Schuster, 1966), p. 239.
13. Ibid.
14. Ibid., p. 240.
15. Mark Twain, *Notebooks & Journals*, vol 3, 1883–1891(Berkeley: University of California Press, 1979), p. 287.
16. Kaplan, p. 239.

Chapter. 6. Mark Twain Fails in Business but Wins in Literature

1. Robert D. Jerome and Herbert A Wisbey, Jr., eds., *Mark Twain in Elmira*, (Elmira, NY: Mark Twain Society, Inc., 1977), pp. 193–195.

2. *Mark Twain's Letters*, vol 1., ed. Albert B Paine (London: Harper & Brothers, 1917), p. 299.

3. Ron Powers, *Mark Twain: A Life* (New York: Free Press, 2005), p. 450.

4. Ibid., p. 459.

5. Ibid., p. 478.

6. Albert B. Paine, *Mark Twain: A Biography* (New York: Harper & Bros., 1912), 2:798.

7. Mark Twain, *Adventures of Huckleberry Finn*, ed. Scully Bradley et. al. (New York: WW. Norton & Company, 1961), p. 13.

8. Ibid.

9. Ibid., p. 19.

10. Ibid., p. 30.

11. Ibid., p. 33.

12. Ibid.

13. Ibid., p. 134.

14. Ibid., p. 153.

15. Ibid., p. 170.

16. Ibid., p. 294.

17. Ibid.

18. Fishkin, quoted in Elaine and Harry Mensh, *Black White & Huckleberry Finn* (Tuscaloosa, AL: University of Alabama Press, 2000), pp. 36–37.

19. Paine, *Mark Twain: A Biography*, vol 2, p. 797.

20. Ibid., p. 221.

21. Ibid., p. 222.

22. Ibid., p. 227.

23. Powers, p. 477.

24. Lyrics can be found on: STlyrics.com2016 Musicblog (/ blog.htm).

25. Robert Louis Stevenson, quoted in Paine, p. 794.

Chapter 7. A Passion for Technology Leads Twain to *A Connecticut Yankee*

1. Forrest Robinson in "Mark Twain: A Brief Biography," *A Historical Guide to Mark Twain* (New York: Oxford University Press, 2002), p. 45.
2. From *Notebooks & Journals*, vol. 3, ed. Robert P. Browning, Michael Frank, and Lin Salamo (Berkeley: University of California Press, 1979), p. 86. Noted in Ron Powers, *Mark Twain: A Life* (New York: Free Press, 2005), p. 498.
3. Shelley Fisher Fishkin, ed., *A Historical Guide to Mark Twain* (New York: Oxford University Press, 2002), p. 269.
4. Ibid.
5. Powers, p. 521.
6. Mark Twain, *A Connecticut Yankee in King Arthur's Court* (New York: Harper & Brothers, 1917), p 132.
7. Ibid., p. 137.
8. Ibid., p. 138.
9. Ibid., pp. 138–139.
10. Ibid., p. 142.
11. Ibid., p. 147.
12. Powers, p. 523.
13. *Connecticut Yankee*, pp. 237–238.
14. Ibid., p. 128.
15 Ibid., p. 129.
16. Ibid., p. 362.
17 Ibid.
18. Ibid., p. 352.
19. Ibid., p. 237.
20. Ibid., pp. 418–419.

21. Jonathan Yardley, "On Mark Twain's 'A Connecticut Yankee in King Arthur's Court,'" *Washington Post*, blog, September 5, 2009.

22. Cari Keebaugh, "The Many Sides of Hank: Modifications, Adjustments,of Mark Twain's *A Connecticut Yankee in King Arthur's Court*," in ImageTxt. Vol 3 No. 3. English.ufl.edu. archives. 23. Ibid.

24. *Connecticut Yankee*, p. 381.

Chapter 8. The Later Life of Samuel Clemens and Writings of Mark Twain

1. Ron Powers, *Mark Twain: A Life* (New York: Free Press, 2005), p. 578.

2. Ibid., p. 617.

3. "The Fence Painter," The Mark Twain Boyhood Home and Museum, November–December 2016, vol. 36, no. 6.

4. Cindy Lovell, Virtual Tour from American History TV C/Span 3, https:www.c-span.org/video/?329486-1/mark-twains-hrtford-home.

5. A letter from 1874, quoted in Robert D. Jerome and Herbert A Wisbey, Jr., eds., *Mark Twain in Elmira* (Elmira, NY: Mark Twain Society, 1977), p. 38.

6. Letter to William Dean Howells, quoted in *Mark Twain in Elmira*, p. 39.

7. Cindy Lovell to the author, letter of December 28, 2016.

8. Author interview with Lovell, December 15, 2016.

LITERARY TERMS

colloquial Having to do with informal conversation; how people talk.

first person In the voice of "I," being told from one person's viewpoint.

imagery Words that paint a picture, describing how something looks, feels, sounds, etc.

irony Language whose meaning is the opposite of what the speaker actually intends.

memoir A true story that a person tells about his or her own life.

omniscient narrator The all-knowing voice that tells the story and is able to know the thoughts of all of the characters.

satire A piece of writing that makes fun of a person or idea.

symbolism Using one thing to stand for, represent, or suggest something else.

theme A distinctive quality or concern in one or more works of fiction.

Major Works by Mark Twain

[Starred books are also suitable for younger readers]

1867 *The Celebrated Jumping Frog of Calaveras County, and Other Sketches**

1869 *The Innocents Abroad, or The New Pilgrim's Progress*

1871 *Mark Twain's (Burlesque) Autobiography*

1872 *Roughing It **

1873 *The Gilded Age: A Tale of Today*

1875 *Mark Twain's Sketches, New and Old **

1876 *The Adventures of Tom Sawyer**

1877 *A True Story and the Recent Carnival of Crime*

1880 *A Tramp Abroad*

1880 *1601–Conversation as it was by the Social Fireside in the Times of the Tudors **

1882 *The Prince and the Pauper: A tale for young people of all ages **

1883 *Life on the Mississippi**

1885 *Adventures of Huckleberry Finn **

1889 *A Connecticut Yankee in King Arthur's Court **

1892 *Merry Tales **

1894 *The Tragedy of Pudd'nhead Wilson, and the Comedy of those Extraordinary Twins*

1894 *Tom Sawyer Abroad **

1896 *Tom Sawyer, Detective **

1896 *Personal Recollections of Joan of Arc*

1897 *Following the Equator*

1900 *The Man that Corrupted Hadleyburg*

1904 *Extracts from Adam's Diary, Translated from the Original MS* *

1906 *Eve's Diary* *

1909 *Is Shakespeare Dead?* *

1909 *Extract from Captain Stormfield's Visit to Heaven*

FURTHER READING

Blaisdell, Bob, ed. *The Wit and Wisdom of Mark Twain: A Book of Quotations*. Mineola, NY: Dover, 2013.

Kerley, Barbara. *The Extraordinary Mark Twain (According to Susy)*. New York: Scholastic, 2010.

Prince, April Jones. *Who Was Mark Twain?* New York: Grosset & Dunlap, 2004.

Rasmussen, R. Ken. *Mark Twain for Kids: His Life and Times*. Chicago: Chicago Review Press, 2004.

WEBSITES

Elmira College: Center for Mark Twain Studies

www.marktwainstudies.com

Virtually tour the grounds of Quarry Farm and access the college's extensive archives of primary and secondary materials.

The Mark Twain Boyhood Home and Museum

www.marktwainmuseum.org

Provides updates on the many events held at the museum in Hannibal, Missouri, as well as information on Twain's life and works.

The Mark Twain House & Museum

www.marktwainhouse.org

Seeks to preserve Twain's legacy through education and exhibitions at the Hartford museum; website includes family background and photographs.

Mark Twain Project Online

www.marktwainproject.org

Contains a comprehensive digital collection of texts, notes, letters, and images.

Mark Twain Quotations, Newspaper Collections, & Related Resources

www.twainquotes.com

Includes a catalog of quotes as well as the full text of articles written by Twain.

INDEX